Condensed Wisdom of Twenty Years of Experience on the Track from the Most Successful Speculator in the History of the American Turf

from the only personal interviews ever given by Pittsburg Phil (George E. Smith), one of the most successful bettors of all time.

RACING MAXIMS & METHODS OF PITTSBURG PHIL

RACING MAXIMS & METHODS OF PITTSBURG PHIL

EDWARD W. COLE

GBC PRESS
P. O. Box 98115
Las Vegas, NV 89193
www.gamblersbookclub.com

TO MR. WALTER KEYS

A loyal and valued friend of Mr. George E. Smith (Pittsburg Phil)
during many years of active business association and comradeship.

Copyright © 1908 by Edward W. Cole
This Edition Copyright © 2012 by Gamblers Book Club
All Rights Reserved

Library of Congress Catalog Number: 2012931118
ISBN 10: 1-58042-314-0   ISBN 13: 978-1-58042-314-4
GBC Press is an imprint of Cardoza Publishing

GBC PRESS
c/o Cardoza Publishing
P.O. Box 98115, Las Vegas, NV 89193
Toll-Free Phone (800)522-1777
email: info@gamblersbookclub.com
www.gamblersbookclub.com

TABLE OF CONTENTS

INTRODUCTION   **11**

THE INSIDE SKINNY ON
    PITTSBURGH PHIL   **13**

PREFACE   **17**

1. **WHAT ONE MUST KNOW TO PLAY
   THE RACES**   **21**
   CHARACTERISTICS OF WINNING HANDICAPPERS 22
   IMPORTANT PERSONAL RULES FOR WINNERS 25

2. **ONE DAY'S WORK AT THE TRACK**   **27**
   EVALUATING A HORSE AT THE TRACK.......................................28
   WHEN THE RACE HAS BEEN RUN 31
   THE IMPORTANCE OF THE JOCKEY...34
   THE IMPORTANCE OF THE TRAINER 36

3. SPECULATION   39
GETTING GOOD INFORMATION 41
KNOWING THE VALUE OF YOUR HORSE 44
GETTING THE BEST PRICE 46

4. HANDICAPPING   49
HORSES MUST BE IN TOP CONDITION 50
START WITH SCALE WEIGHT 52
CLOSELY OBSERVE THE TOTE BOARD 54
THE BIGGEST WIN I EVER ATTEMPTED TO MAKE 55
SPECULATING ON HANDICAP RACES..57
THE TEMPERAMENT OF THE HORSE 59
TRACK CONDITIONS ARE IMPORTANT 60

5. THE FALLACY OF HANDICAPPING BY TIME   63
AN EXCEPTION TO THE FALLACY 65
DO NOT OVERVALUE YOUR OPINIONS 66

6. HANDICAPPING BY CLASS AND WEIGHT   69
CLASSIFYING HORSES 70
THE IMPORTANCE OF WEIGHT..72
THE USE OF STIMULANTS 74

7. THE TREATMENT OF HORSES   77
A HORSE MUST FEEL COMFORTABLE 79

8. WILLIAM COWAN ON PITTSBURGH PHIL   81
BETTING ON CINCINNATUS 82
PITTSBURGH PHIL, DETECTIVE 83

9. HOW PITTSBURGH PHIL GAVE TOD SLOAN HIS START 85

10. ANECDOTES CONCERNING MEN OF FAME WHO WAGERED HUGE SUMS 93

LADY ELIZABETH AND HERMIT..95
SIR GEORGE CHETWYND AND SIR JOHN ASHLEY....................97
THE BROTHERS BALTAZZI...98
JUBILEE JUGGINS AND OTHER PLUNGERS...............................99
THE OTHER ENGLISH RACE GOERS 101

11. DRUGS AND THEIR EFFECT UPON HORSES 103

THE VETERINARIAN'S REPORT ON STIMULANTS 105
COMMON DRUGS USED TO STIMULATE HORSES..................107

12. AN EXPLANATION OF THE TIME AND WEIGHT PERCENTAGE TABLE 111

13. MAXIMS OF PITTSBURGH PHIL: PART 1 119

14. MAXIMS OF PITTSBURGH PHIL: PART 2 121

15. MAXIMS OF PITTSBURGH PHIL: PART 3 125

INTRODUCTION

Pittsburgh Phil is the father of modern handicapping. Long before comprehensive data like that found in *The Daily Racing Form* was available to horse bettors, he invented a system of record keeping that guided him in making business-like wagers on thoroughbred races. He carefully complied statistics on everything related to horse races and, based on his hard-earned information, became the world's best-known handicapper.

In this book you'll discover how a world-class handicapper works his wonders at the betting windows. You'll learn the things to look for at the track, and how to turn your results into hard cash by determining the best bets to make. You'll understand the value of past performance and the secrets of observing more than just the obvious facts before, during and after a race.

What's more, you will be thoroughly entertained by some of the world's best racing anecdotes, each with a valuable lesson. Further, the vintage language that Pittsburgh Phil and Edward W. Cole use in sharing their time-tested secrets and telling their tales from the track is positively priceless—a thoroughly enjoyable change from the dry language often found in handicapping books.

Far more than simply a fascinating read about races run in days of yore, this book has become the "bible" of horse bettors across the world. You'll learn, you'll laugh, you'll live the stories right along with Pittsburgh Phil, the most famous and the smartest thoroughbred handicapper who ever lived.

THE INSIDE SKINNY ON PITTSBURGH PHIL

T. DANA SMITH
Senior Editor, Gambler's Book Club

Astute thoroughbred handicappers like the man I recently met at the Gamblers Book Club in Las Vegas still utter Pittsburgh Phil's name in reverence. "I've read every book ever published on horseracing," he told me, "but the one I learned the most from is *The Racing Maxims and Methods of Pittsburgh Phil.*"

As the book reviewer for the GBC, I felt it my duty to find out all I could about the author of a gambling book that has lasted for over a century. Turns out Pittsburgh Phil is arguably the most famous handicapper of thoroughbred races who ever lived—and his advice remains as valid and valuable today as it was when it was first published in 1908.

Pittsburgh Phil was a pioneer handicapper, a true prodigy who placed his first winning bet on the ponies when he was around 17 years old. That was five years after he started working as a cork cutter for $5 a week to help support his widowed mother and three siblings, saving a little each payday to buy and train gamecocks. Later, he also wagered money on baseball games in the plethora of pool halls that booked bets in Pittsburgh, telling his mother that his winnings had come from raises at the cork factory.

He started focusing his attention on the ponies in the 1870s when he heard a horserace being broadcast over the telegraph in a local pool hall. The fast-paced, vivid spiel of the sportscaster fascinated him. Almost immediately, he was hooked on horses. After a year of recording all the racing statistics he could glean from the broadcasts, he placed his first bet, winning $38. Realizing that he could make more money in a day than he could in six weeks at the factory, he quit his day job and pursued handicapping full time. Over the next couple of years, George E. Smith, Pittsburgh Phil's birth name, earned more than $5,000 from his new profession, most of which he socked away. Now, that may not sound like much of a wage these days, but it sure beat the $260 a year he earned cutting cork. By 1885, at the age of 23, he had won over $100,000—without ever watching a live horserace.

The good news was that he had become one of the most famous gamblers in Pittsburgh. The bad news? He wasn't making as much money as he used to make because he could no longer get the good odds he had gotten when nobody knew him—the odds plummeted because so many people duplicated his betting choices.

What to do?

He moved to Chicago, stopping to watch his first horserace at the 1885 Kentucky Derby along the way. In the Windy City, he became known as a highly successful "plunger," a gambler who bet large sums of money on the horses.

After moving to New York City a few years later, Pittsburgh Phil established Pleasant Valley Stable, buying, selling and racing thoroughbreds. His two most successful steeds were King Cadmus and Parvenue. In this book, he talks about the odds snafu at the track that cost him thousands of dollars in his bets on Parvenue to win. He also hired several jockeys, the most famous being Tod Sloan, who invented the "monkey crouch" racing position. To acquire the services of Sloan, he made him an offer he couldn't refuse—a clever scheme you'll learn about from Pittsburgh Phil himself in these pages.

Through the copious records he kept on every horse, jockey, trainer and track, we learned that Pittsburgh Phil eventually amassed a fortune of $3,250,000 through investing his earnings from the track, the equivalent of about $80 million today. More importantly, in an era when no statistical data were readily available, he invented the first scientific approach to handicapping thoroughbreds. His methods included employing scouts, called "beards" in those days, who reported to him daily and anonymously placed bets for him with the bookmakers, who were reluctant to book any of Phil's bets. In fact, in their efforts to protect themselves, the bookies even hired the Pinkerton detective agency to uncover the identities of his agents.

Pittsburgh Phil's winning methods remained a closely guarded secret until he shared them with his trusted friend, Edward W. Cole, Turf Editor of the *New York Evening Telegram*, in the only interview he ever gave. Three years after George E. Smith's death from tuberculosis at age 43 in 1905, the first edition of this book was published. Before he died, the shy and even-tempered bachelor who had become the world's most famous plunger built his mausoleum in Uniondale Cemetery in Pittsburgh. Standing atop the impressive stone structure is a statue of Pittsburgh Phil holding a racing from—a fitting tribute to the father of modern handicapping.

PREFACE

EDWARD W. COLE
Turf Editor of the New York *Evening Telegram*

Throughout the turf world and the world in general, there live a great many persons who believe that the success of George E. Smith, a.k.a. Pittsburgh Phil, on the racetrack was due more to a run of good luck than to the employment of skillful business methods. I have seen him make wagers at the tracks on the Metropolitan Circuit and win large sums of money. As now and then the amounts of his winnings became known, spectators sighed and wondered why they could not have been so "lucky" as this clear-headed young man who hailed from the busiest city of Pennsylvania.

It was not luck that won a fortune for Pittsburgh Phil. It was the application of one of the shrewdest minds that ever undertook to make racing a business and not a gambling uncertainty. There were times when Pittsburgh Phil might have been lucky for a moment, as everybody engaged in business is lucky at some time or another. But for the most part, the bulk of his fortune was obtained because he went about the matter of racing on a strictly business basis, and gave exactly as much and similar attention to it as the prosperous broker or banker gives to his.

The particular value of this work is that it contains the only personal interviews that Pittsburgh Phil ever gave to any man in regard to the proper methods to be applied to cope with racing and its various emergencies. Although hundreds tried to interview him at one time or another, he refused absolutely to say anything regarding his manner of handling his wagers, his channels of obtaining information, or the system he applied to make race speculation worth as much to him as stock speculation is worth to the broker.

To this writer he talked freely. At various times he entered exhaustively into the plans he had made on various occasions and the methods he had used to be successful in his business. He considered it as much a legitimate business as trading in cotton or oil. He scoffed at the notion that any one could win on the turf purely by luck, and said that the man who would be successful should be able not only to know his horses, but to know the methods of those who were engaged in the direct control of the horses. Further than that he insisted that one must study the bookmakers and their methods. This volume explains how he managed his affairs so as to win a fortune of more than $1,700,000, by knowledge of the subject with which he was dealing.

George E. Smith was one of the quietest men who ever lived in connection with American turf affairs. When others would be inclined to boast of their success, Smith would shrink from publicity. He would fairly run at the sight of a reporter if he thought one was coming to question him about his prosperity. He began as a cork cutter in Pittsburgh. That life was slow and dreary, and he made up his mind early that he would get away from it. He had no fixed plan as to what he would do, but he once remarked rather dryly that he thought he could do a little better than cutting corks, inasmuch as he knew how to divide six by two. He was a man of exemplary habits, very fond of his immediate relatives, and never forgetful of a friend.

His first speculation was in baseball. At one time there was not a little betting in Pittsburgh on the national game, a practice that afterward dropped out of fashion. In any event, at this particular period, Pittsburgh Phil gathered some ready cash and came to the East to study racetrack methods. He did not begin to speculate on the turf extensively until he was well posted, and had become well versed in a great deal of valuable information through experience. He began betting with the proverbial shoestring. Then he continued the business that proved so successful until a short time prior to his death.

This book tells plainly and simply how Pittsburgh Phil managed his affairs to accumulate a fortune. Some of it is almost in his exact language, but all of it is authorized and direct. In its way, this is a novel addition to turf literature, and it is quite probable that if you are interested in the turf, you will find a great many hints that will be of assistance to you in the future.

Doubtless many of you will perceive that speculation on races is not so much blind guessing as it is applied study to the hundred and one details that are necessary to be successful.

Now, let us hear from Pittsburgh Phil himself.

1
WHAT ONE MUST KNOW TO PLAY THE RACES

Playing the races appears to be the one business in which men believe they can succeed without special study, special talent or special exertion. For that reason the bookmakers ride around in automobiles and eat at Delmonico's while the majority of regular race-goers jokingly congratulate themselves on being lucky if they have the price of a meal and carfare.

Why a man who is sensible in other things holds this idea I have never been able to satisfy myself. He knows and will acknowledge that such methods would mean failure to him as a merchant, a broker, or businessman in any other walk of life, but he never seems to apply that knowledge to racing. It must be that the quick action hypnotizes him, or the excitement dazzles him, or that he thinks himself too lucky to lose. I never could tell exactly which.

Many men are playing the races nowadays and the majority of them are losing. Some are winning, however, and while they are few, they are the characters that we must analyze and whose methods we must study if we would succeed as they do. Seldom does one hear anything about these men until facts are studied below the surface at the racetrack. Then you hear everything about them. They are envied; they are called lucky; they are said to be men who always have some unfair advantage in a race. In fact you hear all reports about them except the truth.

I am not puffing the plunger in this class. The one who does that is the man who accumulates a bankroll one day only to lose it the next. He is the comet of the racing world. He lights up everything one minute and the next minute he "lights out." Think it over yourself and count on your fingers the names of the men who have made the flashlight bankrolls at the track.

Where are they now?

Few can answer. There is no comparison between them and the good solid speculator who studies and works hard to ensure success.

CHARACTERISTICS OF WINNING HANDICAPPERS

Concerning the class that I mentioned above, the class that includes the men who quit winners year after year, one seldom hears of them until able to separate all the elements that make up racing. They are orderly, decent and quiet. They go about their business without bluster. They are calm, no matter how much excitement may be around them, for they are only there for business. They would have succeeded, I believe, had they turned their talents in some other direction than toward racing. When you have analyzed their mental force, you will have found men who are cool, deliberate in action, men of strong will power and of a philosophical nature. You will find that all have energy and the bulldog trait of sticking to one idea. You will find them exceedingly quick in sizing up a situation and just as quick to take advantage of it. It does not matter what their breeding may be, their birth or training afterwards—if they have these talents they are almost certain to be men of success. They have gone a long way toward winning before they ever began to bet.

A man who has not an opinion of his own and the ability to stick to it in the face of all kinds of arguments—and argument includes betting odds in a race—has not one chance in a million to beat the races for any length of time. One who is susceptible to tips, or what is known as paddock information, may get along very well for a while, but I have yet to find one who has stuck to this line who could show a bankrollof any dimension.

Men like Charles Heaney, W. Beverley, "Mattie" Corbett, "Cad" Irish, "Pack" McKenna, "Ike" Hakelburg and others of their class, all exceedingly successful handicappers, never think of seeking information as a basis for their betting. They rely upon their own judgment entirely and never form that judgment until after the most careful consideration. To them paddock and stable information is only an incident to confirm their previous judgment. Frequently I have met half a dozen owners and trainers of horses that have been entered in the same race and each has told me that his horse could not lose. I therefore had a half a dozen tips on the same race, and it was there that my own judgment stood me in good stead.

Now, what do the form players and successful handicappers know about horses?

Well, I might say, incidentally, that they know the capabilities of every good horse in training and have an accurate idea of what he will do under all circumstances. They know his habits and his disposition as well, and perhaps better than you know your own brother. They know when he is at his best and when otherwise. They know what weather suits him, what track he likes best, what distance he likes to go, what weight he likes to carry, and what kind of a jockey he likes to have on his back. They know what the jockeys can do and what they cannot do, and in addition to that, they are close observers in the betting ring. If there is anything wrong, it generally shows in the market.

Does not that mean some study? Can a man who regards racing as easy, who spends only an hour or so looking up the "dope," figuring upon horses as they would on a piece of machinery by time and weight, know as much as they do? It takes them years of constant close, cool-headed observation to acquire this knowledge; and even at that, the returns are often meager.

I have said that they know the horses. By this I do not mean that they know all the horses racing. The smartest player does not know every horse that runs any more than he bets on every race. He pays attention only to the better class of horses. The others that win only once or twice a year, he dismisses from his calculation. He knows that upon the money lost on bad horses the bookmaker thrives. But as soon as one of these horses from the rear rank shows any consistent form, he is added to the list of representative horses and is thereafter considered. Being possessed of an extraordinary memory, I can keep all the information I need about a horse in my head. Not all of the men I am speaking of can do this. I can recall a long past race vividly, every detail of it, the weight carried, the distance, the condition of it, and every incident that happened during the running. Few can do this so they have substituted a system of bookkeeping by which they accomplish a similar result.

I have said that a player of the races must be philosophical. He must not get upset by a series of winnings any more than by a succession of losses. The minute a man loses his balance on the racetrack he is like a horse that is trying to run away. He gets rattled. He throws discretion to the wind. If he is winning, he simply believes that he cannot lose and immediately afterward gets a bump that may put him out of business. If he is losing, he becomes the prey of every kind of information and influence. I have known men who bet thousands of dollars on a race when in that state of mind—men who play a "tip" given to them by a boy who sells chewing gum, a castoff stable boy, or a bartender. It has been my observation that the best thing for a man in that condition to do is to leave the track entirely and take a vacation amid other scenes.

Racing is not going to stop tomorrow nor next week. It is going on somewhere in the United States three hundred and thirteen days in the year. He can come back and there will be plenty of money for him to win, if he can win it.

IMPORTANT PERSONAL RULES FOR WINNERS

One of the important rules of the men who win at the racetrack is that they must have absolute freedom from distraction and interference of all kinds. The successful race player knows there is a bar and a cafe at the track, and that there are some very interesting conversationalists to be met with every few steps—but he has no time for either the bar or the funny storytellers. I may appear to be exceedingly cold blooded, but for the benefit of my friends, I must say that a man who wishes to be successful cannot divide his attention between horses and women. A man who accepts the responsibility of escorting a woman to the racetrack and seeing that she is comfortably placed and agreeably entertained, cannot keep his mind on his work before him. Between races, a man has enough to do without replying to the questions asked by her.

This is of so much importance to me that it has only been upon very rare occasions, and then in Saratoga, that I have asked even my mother to accompany me. Upon such days, the card showed to me that there was little chance for speculation and I would, therefore, be free to devote my time otherwise. A sensible woman understands this and cannot feel hurt at my words. I do not wish to say that she should not be permitted to enter the racetrack. On the contrary, she is an addition and an adornment to a beautiful scene, and she should always be welcome. But if you are going to make a business of betting, you must not let a thought for anything else interfere.

All consistently successful players of horses are men of temperate habits in life. Speculation on the turf, as in all other kinds of business, requires the best efforts of its devotees. You cannot sit up all night, drink heavily, and dissipate otherwise and expect to win money at the racetrack. You could not do it in Wall Street and you could not do it running a store, so why do you expect to do it there? I do not mean that you are not to have any diversion whatever. Healthful recreation and relaxation are just as necessary to the race player as to any other businessman. If a man does not get it, he becomes what in turf vernacular would be called "brain sour." If a horse is continually worked and raced, he loses his speed, health and ambition and has to be freshened with a rest. He is "track sour" and stale.

It is exactly the same with a man, and he will realize it sooner or later.

I have spoken this way about what kind of man I think the successful race player should be. I have not touched on the morality of playing the races because I do not think it is under discussion. Some men may say, or think, that racing attended by betting has a harmful influence. I have nothing to say about that. There must be speculation in every branch of business, whether it is racing or keeping a dry goods store. In that respect all business may be said to have a harmful effect also. The ethics of the question do not concern me.

Speculating upon racing was the one thing that I believed I was best fitted to do, and therefore I did it. I have no regrets or apologies to offer.

2
ONE DAY'S WORK
AT THE TRACK

There is no better way of making plain what a successful racing man is than to tell of his day at the track. What he does and what he will not do. How he conducts himself. How he remains always master of the situation and of himself. It seems to me that will be the best kind of a lesson for the man who would like to share with him in his general prosperity.

Preparation for a day at the track begins the night before, of course, for then the entries of the day ate studied, impossibilities are eliminated, and the contenders are decided upon. This is succeeded by an early retirement in a condition that will guarantee natural rest from the fatigue of the day at hand. The excitement and nervous strain of the incidents of the previous day are to be dismissed from the mind, and sleep is to be wooed without a rival.

As a result, the racing man should arise in the morning, cool and clearheaded, and with the first opening of his eyes he should again take up the problem of the day. The horses come before him at once and they never leave until after the contest is decided. I think about them the very first thing when I awaken, weighing them in one light and from one standpoint and another. As I dress and eat my breakfast, I am placing them here and there, giving each a chance until at last, from all standpoints, I decide which one, in a truly and perfectly run race, devoid of the hundred or more unlooked for incidents that can happen, should be the winner. In this frame of mind I go to the track.

EVALUATING A HORSE AT THE TRACK

Once I enter the gate it is all business with me, and my program of one day does not change. I get the names of the jockeys and the positions of the horses at the post if it is a race in which I believe there is a fair speculative opportunity. I know, of course, the kind of day it is and the condition of the track. I next go up into the grandstand and watch the horses warming up. This is of the utmost importance, for although my mind may be centered on two or possibly three horses, at the same time it is important that I watch the others for fear there may be an unexpected display of form in any of them. If I do not see any of the horses warm up that I had in mind, I immediately go to the paddock, after having my agent bring me the betting quotations. Arriving there I devote my time and attention entirely to the contenders, as I have picked them, and to nothing else.

It is impossible to overestimate the value of this ability to tell the condition of a thoroughbred. It is the twin sister of handicapping and more important. In that respect, the ordinary form handicapper is, so to say, handicapped. What may appear to be right on paper very, very often is wrong in the paddock. This ability to tell whether a horse is at its best before a race is acquired only after years of the closest kind of study. The merest tyro can tell in a race whether a horse is doing its best, but when it comes to getting a knowledge of what he can be expected to do before a race from a blanketed animal walking about the paddock or standing in his stall, special knowledge is necessary. It is not a talent. A man is not born with it; he must acquire it by hard work and close observation. He must be able to decide whether a horse is in good condition or not, whether he appears to feel like running a race or otherwise.

If a horse looks dull in the eye, dry, or moves and acts sluggishly, in the majority of cases it is to me almost a sure sign that he is not at his best. I say a majority of cases because there are exceptions to every rule and some of the best horses we have ever bred had no more animation apparently than a "night hawk" cab horse before a contest. Some of these horses need only a warm up gallop on the way to the post to get out of their dull condition.

You often see a jockey ride at top speed after the parade in front of the grandstand to the starting judge, and you may usually depend upon it that it is for livening purposes. Frequently, trainers want to deceive the public as to the condition of the horse by having it appear dull and of little account in the paddock. This helps in the betting. It is not an unfair strategy because to them it is just as important to win a bet as it is to you and me. It is here that your knowledge of the disposition of a horse will stand you in good stead. If you have studied him properly you will know whether he needs the usual warm up, a preliminary gallop of a quarter of a mile, or a sprint of an eighth, or again simply a jog to the post.

An inspection of the horses in the paddock pays me for another reason. It tells of the nervous condition of a horse. Nerves are as important to a horse in training as to a person engaged in any physical contest. Poor nerves are indicated by fretting. A horse that frets is a very dangerous betting proposition. I can illustrate this by one particular instance in which a horse showed to me distinctly that he would not be able to repeat the high-class race of a short time before. This was a horse called Pulsus. In my calculations, I became convinced that, all other things being favorable, he would have an excellent chance to win.

Pulsus did not warm up for the race I have in mind, so I went into the paddock to see him. I was surprised at his appearance. He was as nervous as a horse could possibly be. He had "broken out," so that the perspiration was literally running off his skin in a stream. My eyes told me that he had lost at least one hundred pounds in weight since his last race, and was certainly not within twenty-five pounds of his previous form, simply through nervous strain in his stall and the excitement in the paddock. Pulsus was one of the favorites that day. I forget just what price they were taking, but I know that it was less than two to one. I made up my mind that I would not play him straight, or to place, at a thousand to one, so I looked elsewhere for the winner. I instructed a bookmaker to lay against Pulsus for me straight and place for a considerable sum of money. The result was a fair winning, as Pulsus was nowhere. His energy and stamina gone, he finished back in the ruck.

Having inspected the three horses, or whatever number I have in mind, as possible contenders, I discover perhaps that one or two of them, in my opinion, are not in the most promising condition to run a winning race. The scene of my operations shifts immediately from the paddock to the betting ring. I find there that the favorite is one of the horses whose looks did not impress me in the paddock. It is here that the first exercise of will power begins. There is something about a favorite that seems to sway players to bet upon him. In many cases their own judgment tells them that the horse in question is in a false position, but they become afraid of themselves. A majority of players will fancy that particular horse, and the individual will begin to wonder if his judgment is right. Just as the evening newspapers publish a consensus of the opinions of the newspaper handicappers, so the prices in the ring is publishing the consensus of the best handicappers at the track. It takes a strong man to disregard this, but I have always done so without any hesitation.

No matter what the class, the previous performances, or the prestige of the horse that has been played into favoritism, or the stable to which it belongs or the jockey that is to ride, or of the money bet upon it, I look elsewhere for the winner if he does not suit me. Mechanically I take up the second choice and subject it to as severe a handicapping test as was the winner, and if the second choice fails to come up to the standard, I pass it by just as willingly as I did the first. Prices and public opinion have absolutely no influence upon me at this time. I have gone down a list of entries until I have reached a horse that was possibly a rank outsider in the opinion of experts. Upon that horse I pin my faith and upon that horse I bet my money if other circumstances justify me.

Men have often wondered how I could play a third or fourth choice in the race. It was simply because my judgment commanded me to do it. I may have been wrong, but after the race I knew why I was wrong. It was costly knowledge, but it was not useless because it would serve me some other day.

WHEN THE RACE HAS BEEN RUN

The race is run, let us say. The shouts of the winners and the groans of the losers die away. From the grandstand there comes a rush of men on their way to the betting ring, some to cash their wagers and others to make wagers on the next race. The horses that have been the object of all their hopes a minute before are forgotten by the multitude. They are pulled up on the back stretch, turn and canter back to the stewards, the

jockeys dismount by permission, and the animals are turned over to their handlers with no more than a little perfunctory applause from the grandstand.

I say the multitude in general has forgotten, but there are some men at the track to whom this period is of the utmost importance. You will see these men along the rail close to the judges' stand, or up in the grandstand with their eyes glued to their field glasses. I have heard the uninformed say, when observing this, "That man is still running the race." It is not necessary to reply to such remarks for time is too precious.

I want to know how a horse pulls up after a race, how the effort has affected him, whether he won easily without calling upon his reserve power, or whether he was distressed and all out. Many a time one horse has beaten another by a length or two, but with an expenditure of effort that told while the beaten horse was not palpably distressed. It will take considerable time for the winner to recover from his effort. The second horse will be improved by the race. The physical make up of horses has much to do with this. There are some light barreled horses, mares particularly, that feel the effects of a race more than others. Suppose such a mare were entered in a race two or three days later against practically the same field. Being convinced that the strain had told, I might bet on the horse that ran second or even third, other conditions being favorable.

When I have won after such procedure, I have been accused by some of having what they term "an ace in the hole." That is, they have accused me of having had jockeys pull a horse in one race to make a killing in the next, when it is nothing in the world but my close observation after the previous race had been run.

During the running of the race my glasses never leave the horses engaged. I see every move they make. I can see that this one is not in his stride, or is running unnaturally, or is being ridden poorly. I can see if a horse is sulking, what horse is fit, what horse is unfit. After the race is run, it is sometimes said that a horse has had a bad ride, or that the trainer has sent him to the post in an unfit condition, or anything and everything—except the truth.

Knowing the disposition of all the good horses, I am able to say pretty clearly that the failure of a horse to do better was due to chance or unintelligent handling, perfectly innocent in themselves. Possibly the jockey had given him a cut of the whip at the post, which made him sour; possibly the track did not suit him. His post position, the size of the field or a bump in a jam may have taken away his courage. He may have been bumped on the start, shut off, pocketed, roughed, or interfered with in a dozen ways. Whatever it was, I tried to locate the trouble and record it for the future.

Take an illustration of this: Eugenia Burch was a mare that would run an exceptionally good race if she could have an outside position and was not bothered in any way. It was this fact that made her somewhat erratic in her running. In a small field and with an outside position, she could be expected to show her best form. She could run around her field very impressively. She was naturally a slow beginner and she always had to go around her field. Now, if she were in a big field and had an inside position where she would be bumped and knocked about in the early stages, she would never extend herself until the coast was clear, and then it was usually too late. Thus, she had been beaten often by horses inferior to her, and there had been some comment on that fact by persons who did not understand the mare. I think she was timid and in that particular, she was like some jockeys I have known. They will ride much better on the outside than they will in the middle of a bunch. I am glad to say that such riders are in a minority, but they exist just the same. It is for you to find out who they are and to classify them for future consideration. On the other hand, the majority of the horses and riders are game and will fight for victory no matter where they are placed.

While speaking about this, I can recall seeing horses fight their way through a field irrespective of conditions, ridden at the same time by a timid boy. The spectacle was as disheartening to me as it must have been to the horse itself. I have seen a good, game horse striving with all his heart, fighting his rider to allow him to push into a space that only his trained eye told him gave him a chance for victory. I have seen these horses plough between two other horses and spread them apart, as a giant football rusher will do with only the goal in his mind. Gold Heels was that kind of horse. He was always fighting. No matter where he was or what were the surrounding conditions, he was doing his work like a bulldog. He was never daunted and he never stopped until his physical powers failed. Gold Heels was the "bear;" Eugenia Burch was the other extreme.

THE IMPORTANCE OF THE JOCKEY

This calls to mind another horse that may be said to illustrate another phase of the case. Previous belonged to M. F. Dwyer, and he was good and game as a horse could be, but there were times when nothing could induce Previous to extend himself. Those times were when Willie Simms was on his back. Simms was one of the best jockeys this country ever knew, but somehow or other, he and Previous could not agree. The rider could use every art he knew, every wile and stratagem, but Previous would not get away at the post, would not run, and would not extend himself. Put a stable boy on the same horse and Previous could be depended upon to run a good race; and when Tod Sloan rode him, he would always do his best.

I mention Tod Sloan. In my opinion he was possibly the greatest rider the world ever knew on a sulking horse. I have seen him mount the sourest, sulkiest, most intractable horses in training and have seen them run kindly from beginning to end. He had a happy knack of getting acquainted with a horse as soon as he got on its back. He has always told me that he catered to the disposition of his mount, by allowing it to do as it pleased so long as it was in a good position. His maxim was to hold a horse well together, reserving as much speed as possible for the last moment. On the subject of jockeys, I have discovered that there are some who excel on heavy tracks. This may appear strange to the average reader, but it is credible when we remember that there are riders so chicken hearted that if they get hit in the face by a lump of mud, they give up all hope of winning. The other boys go on just as determined as ever.

Skeets Martin was and is a good mud rider. It was this knowledge that caused me to put him up on Howard Mann, which won the Brooklyn Handicap, beating my other two entries, Belmar and The Winner. Tod Sloan was riding for me then and he knew that Howard Mann could beat good horses in the mud, but he did not think he could outstep Belmar. I believed that Howard Mann could beat Belmar under certain conditions and told Martin so. I believed Martin was better than Sloan in the mud, and when Sloan chose the mount on Belmar, I was secretly pleased. The only orders I gave in the race were for Martin to get up on Howard Mann, get off, and go on about his business. I added in a joking way that if Tod were within hearing distance of him at the head of the stretch to tell him to hurry home or he would be too late. Whether Skeets ever said it I do not know, but if he did, Tod never heard him—Howard Mann was half way home before Belmar hit the quarter pole.

In his day at the track, the observing player should give a good deal of attention to jockeys. It can be seen that it is not a bad idea to do this. It was worth something to know the capabilities of Martin in the Brooklyn Handicap over a muddy track as well as it was to know the capabilities of a horse. Howard Mann might have won with a less resolute rider, but with Martin up, his chances for winning were vastly better; consequently there was greater assurance of winning a much larger wager than otherwise. A good rider, a good horse, a good bet—that was one of my mottoes.

A good mud rider will frequently bring a bad horse home, because the riders of the good horses are not as game as they might be. Weak boys are always handicapped on a heavy track. At such a time, a horse needs help to keep him from sprawling and from wasting the energy that will be useful later. It is the same way with a horse that needs to be hard driven. A strong rider must be given the preference in such cases. I have frequently bet on an inferior horse with a strong boy up. Many times an even money favorite has a weak boy up, a boy unable to hold him together. At such a time it is a good opportunity for a strong and strenuous interview with our sworn enemies, the bookmakers. It is a good time to look for long shots. And if you are fortunate enough to be in a position to do so, get a bookmaker to lay against the favorite for you. It is sure money nineteen times out of twenty. It is different, of course, in a free running horse. There, the jockey has comparatively little to do and the disposition of the boy does not help so much. All a rider has to do is to sit still and hold his mount together.

THE IMPORTANCE OF THE TRAINER

There is one other thing that a man should take into consideration in his day in the track, and that is the disposition of the trainers. We have talked about the disposition of the horse and the jockey; and now, about the man who has to do with preparing the horse to race. Of course, you must know who the trainer is, what his connections are, learn his habits and his practices. Even that is not good enough. You must know what his methods are with reference to jockeys.

It is a remarkable fact that honest horses ridden by honest boys are oftentimes beaten by honest trainers. By that, I mean that there are hundreds of occasions when trainers and owners give instructions to their riders that mean sure defeat, although the instructions are given with the best intention in the world. I have seen scores of horses beaten because their riders were told, for example, to keep up with the leaders at any cost. I have seen others choked to death because the jockeys have been instructed to lay away a length or two from the pacemakers. Such incidents are an everyday occurrence and add another element of uncertainty to a most uncertain game at best.

One thing must never be forgotten: A jockey of brains and understanding, while he will ride to orders as far as possible, will exercise his own judgment in case things are not turning out exactly as the owner or trainer anticipated. It is a poor owner or trainer who feels resentment when a capable boy does this. This trait is what helps to make up a high-class jockey. Isaac Murphy, Jimmy McLaughlin, Garrison, Skeets Martin, Tod Sloan, Willie Shaw and boys of their class needed, or need, few instructions. They are required to be told the disposition of the horse only, whether sluggish, a sulker or a free runner, and how the whip should be used. Loading them down with further orders was like putting on more weight, for in their efforts to follow instructions they were bound to jeopardize their chances of winning.

I once heard something that a jockey said to a trainer who had dealt out a spasm of orders that would have filled an almanac: "Say, boss, don't you think you had better have those instruction printed in big type so I can read them as the race is being run? I could not remember what you have said to me if I sat up all night to study them, and this race is going to be over in less than two minutes."

The trainer got a little angry at this and proceeded to call the boy down until the boy suggested that if he were told to do the best he could to win, the stable would have a better chance of taking down the purse. The trainer thought for a minute and peevishly remarked: "Oh, do what you like." Then he walked away.

"Them is the best orders any rider with a good horse under him could get," commented the boy as the line formed for the parade.

It is almost unnecessary to tell what happened in that particular race. The boy was a good boy and he used his judgment. He won in a drive by a neck, and he was on the third best horse in the race at that. Had he been hampered by the instructions originally given, I do not believe he would have finished in the money. It pays you to know the trainers, for their habits will sometimes put you on a good thing at a good price.

Your day at the track, it can be seen, has been a busy day. There has been no idle moment; there has been no time for friendly conversation, good stories, refreshment at the bar, or social meetings. When the last race is over, if you have speculated on two or more events, you will be as tired as if you had been engaged in manual labor for many hours. You will need rest and time for your nerves to become normal. As I stated at the outset, that rest cannot be gained by late hours or dissipation of any kind, but by a sane, temperate, normal course of living.

3
SPECULATION

The betting ring is the center around which racing as a speculation revolves. If there were no betting, there would be no racing, at least as we know it today. I do not propose to enter into a discussion of the ethics of the question when I am going to treat it as a business. Such it has been to me for some years and to many other men.

Sufficient knowledge to tell when to bet, or when not to bet, or when to bet heavily is of paramount importance to every man at the track. This is based upon his knowledge of the horses, their owners, their jockeys and everything connected with them. You may know that a horse or a jockey is at its best. If you have not this knowledge, you will lose many a foolish bet.

The basis of all betting is the amount of profit to be obtained on an investment. That is, every bettor should have such a definite conclusion as to the probable result of the race so that he can form for himself the market value of all horses in a race, and make a schedule of the prices as they should be in his opinion. I regard this as one of the reasons why I have been successful. To explain: There is a field of six or eight horses. I figure and handicap those that have a winning chance. I then fix the odds that appear to me to be legitimate quotations. Possibly one of these horses is quoted at eight to five, another at three to one, and so on down the list. When the bookmakers put up their quotations, it has happened that my prices and the ring prices differ. In one particular case the horse that I had quoted at three to one was a favorite at seven or eight to five when the betting opened. That called for a revision of my own figures, and I handicapped the horses again to see if the error was the bookmaker's or mine.

I considered each horse with regard to the particular race, the weight it carried, the distance and all other conditions, the jockeys and the stable connection. Sometimes it developed that there was a quiet report of one particular horse being "wrong." Such a report always sent me to the paddock where I inspected the horse myself. If satisfied that it was in good condition, I would return to the ring where I and my agents watched the doings of certain men whom I considered it necessary to observe at that particular time on account of their friendly connections with stables. If my agents reported that no liberties were being taken by the men who would do such a thing if everything was not legitimate, I could generally figure whether my quotation or the ring quotation was right. If I could get a bookmaker to bet me three to one or more against a horse winning that should, in my opinion, be no better than eight to five, it was a good investment in my judgment. Upon occasions of that kind, I have made my largest wagers. And I may say without egotism that my deductions were correct, so far as the scale of prices was concerned, seven times out of ten. Of course, I was wrong sometimes; no man is infallible.

Take the reverse of the race of which I have just spoken. In the first instance, I made my largest wagers. But where the horse I fancied was at a price a shade less than I thought it should be, I made the most modest bet. I always financed my money to the best advantage, investing much heavier when I believed I was getting a better price than I had quoted in my own mind against a certain horse. Few men knew how hard I worked during the racing season, and it was in the betting ring that my hardest work was done. It was no easy matter to watch every move of the market just as the big financiers do in Wall Street, but I had to do it.

GETTING GOOD INFORMATION

To get all the data that I wanted before betting on a race, I frequently employed half a dozen men at one time. I have supplemented their labors by an acquaintance with the runners and commissioners who ply between the paddock and the ring. I knew by sight every betting commissioner on the racetracks, whom he represented, and how heavily he bet. This knowledge was possessed by the men who worked for me. They were always on the watch for some clue to the purposes of persons who might have an important influence on the race. As a result of this, there was a never-ending fight of stratagem and ruse during the day. If I had watched them, I knew they had watched me.

Many a time, for instance, I have seen a commissioner come into the ring and bet possibly $500 on a certain horse with a certain bookmaker, after which he would bet $100 or so with other men. Immediately the whisper would go about the ring that "so and so commissioner was betting on such and such a horse." The unthinking and uninformed usually took that as sufficient reason for following the lead. It is here that the fine work began.

My man would stand at the book where the commissioner had bet his $500 and watch the effect of that wager. He would be able to tell in a few minutes. Many a time the same bookmaker has accepted the money, say at three to one, and immediately laid the top price in the ring against the same horse. That would satisfy me. It was a bet for effect. There was collusion between the bookmaker and the commissioner, which would have to be thrown out of the betting calculation altogether. It was intended to trap the unsuspecting public and, I regret to say that it frequently succeeded. Nine times out of ten, such horses do not finish in the money. But such things do not happen frequently; in fact, in these days of racing they are a rare occurrence.

The advantage of this particular incident to me was that it eliminated a possible contender, and in a four- or five-horse race, that had an important effect. It even helped me at times in beating the race on the Dutch book system. Knowing that one horse out of four, say, was not good, I would bet on all the others, in some cases winning twenty-five cents for every dollar invested. In other words, I bought their dollar notes for seventy-five cents each.

I recall one instance, some years ago, of the value of close observation in the betting ring. This occurred when "Mike" Dwyer was the heaviest bettor on the turf. I will not give the names of the other persons concerned for the reason that some of them are now men highly respected who have lived down anything that they might have done in days gone by. The race I allude to was run at a track in the vicinity of New York City, and it was practically a two-horse affair, one of the horses being owned by the Dwyer Brothers, then partners in the best stable of horses that was ever trained. To hide the identity of those concerned in the affair more thoroughly, I will designate the horses as "K and "B." I may say that the incident was about the most cowardly piece of highway robbery that ever occurred in this or any other country.

SPECULATION

The race looked such a certainty for the Dwyer horse, which I will designate "K, that when the betting opened, it was a one to four shot. Few cared to speculate at those odds; consequently the business in the ring was light. I never dreamed of making a bet that day and had dismissed the race from my mind when, as I strolled toward the paddock to look over the horses entered in the following race, I met Charley Dwyer, who was then quite a youngster. We exchanged greetings and I said that it was a walk over for his father's horse. The boy replied that his father was of the same opinion and had just given an order that $30,000 be bet on the horse at any old price.

I do not know what prompted me to go back to the betting ring. Possibly it was curiosity to notice the effect of a $30,000 commission on a horse already held at one to four. To my surprise, there was little or no change noticeable in the odds. The commission had evidently not yet been placed and I began to watch more closely. The horses were called to the post, and still there was no change—one to four was obtainable all over the ring, while the contender showed signs of support from some quarters. In those days, and in these days too, a thirty thousand dollar-commission would or will drive a one to four shot to at least one to seven. There was something awry.

My mind worked quickly: That commission was being held out. The man or men holding it out would do so only with the knowledge that the jockey riding the favorite was in on their conspiracy. I may say right here, in justice to one of the most reputable men on the turf, that this jockey was not Jimmy McLaughlin. As soon as I reached this conclusion, I bet several thousand dollars on the horse designated "B." The race was run and Mr. Dwyer's horse was beaten. His thirty thousand dollars had gone into the hands of some unscrupulous men and a jockey. I never said a word to him and it is possible that he never knew the truth of the affair. A funny part of this whole transaction is that other men, men who had caught the drift of things, have since accused me of being implicated in the plot because my wagers had been the heaviest. But the facts are as I have related. My betting was due solely to my close observation of the ring's proceedings.

In contrast to the foregoing, I can say that I have oftentimes been influenced by a certain person's betting $100 on a certain horse, although hundreds of thousands of dollars of so called wise money may have gone on others in the same race. To me, that hundred dollars represented the confidence of a conservative owner or trainer, and was wagered only after a shrewd mind had drawn a careful conclusion. Hence it is not always the heaviest commission that counts, any more than it is the flashiest horse or the flashiest stable.

KNOWING THE VALUE
OF YOUR HORSE

Financing your capital is one of the secrets of success on the track. You must learn to know the value of your horse. There have been times when I have bet $20,000 and at other times I hesitated about betting $100, although the figures might show that the two horses were equally probable winners. It all depends. And upon that little sentence hangs a world of worry and work in a maelstrom of excited humanity, the betting ring. If the ring is active with smart money coming from every quarter, and if the price offered is genuine, then fall in line with a good wager if the horse being bet upon is a true performer.

There is one individual highly important to every man who bets on horses—a "clocker"—but he must be an expert and he must be honest or he will ruin you. I notice that much has been printed recently of early morning trials at the various tracks, but I would not place too much dependence on these reports where one man pretends to have clocked, say, fifty horses in one morning. To have recognized them, and to have got their time accurately as he is pretending, is an absurdity. Better pass that kind of information over to somebody else if you cannot get the services of a good man who will go to a track with the definite purpose of finding out how the best horses are coming along, and then report honestly. The clocker is something like the scout in the army. He is on the battlefield hours before the main body arrives. He learns when a horse is doing good work, when a horse is getting too much work, and when he is sulking; and that all helps.

It has frequently been as much to my advantage to know when a horse is track sore as it is to know when he is rounding to form. Possibly, a horse has gone off becomes a favorite in a race. That gives me what is called a good "lay." That is an opportunity for me to bet that he does not win. My acquaintance with bookmakers enabled me to do this by having them bet my money for me against the public. With this knowledge, I also have whipsawed a race if there were but two contenders. Knowing one was wrong, I laid against him and bet on the other, beating it both ways. A game of hide and seek goes on in the betting ring. I have told the story of the $500-bet made to get the public to follow a horse that was not meant to win. I have made $500 bets in a ring on horses that I knew could not win, but my motive was to get the better of the market.

The bookmakers are not in the business for their health, and as soon as they learn that certain persons fancy a certain horse and are betting upon it, they shorten the odds upon that horse. It happens that sometimes I have been compelled to use strategy to obtain fair odds upon what I considered to be a possible winner. At times, I have bet $500 or more on horses that I verily believed did not have a chance, simply to have the rumor get about that Pittsburgh Phil was betting on such and such a horse. It has sometimes had the effect I wanted. The price of the horse I knew could not win would shorten and the price of the horse I really fancied would lengthen. It was then that my commissioners would get busy on the dark horse, betting possibly $6,000 or $7,000 dollars. I may have lost a thousand dollars or so on the strategy bet, but the odds on the other more than made up for that. When the pool rooms were running in great numbers, it was possible to get a good bet down in the city and I have frequently played the institution in the city against the other at the racetrack. For instance, I would bet a thousand or more dollars at the track on some horse for a place. My betting would reduce the odds on one horse and raise the price on the other. In the city, my commissioners would get into action and in a few minutes, the telephone and personal interviews would enable them to wager a large amount of money at a fair price on the horse that I believed would win.

GETTING THE BEST PRICE

You cannot be a successful horseplayer if you are going to get the worst of the price all the time. It has taken a whole lot of maneuvering for me to keep even with the several hundred shrewd bookmakers. I know they have trailed me and my men everywhere on the track and off. They wanted to know everything that I did and was going to do. That never made me mad because it was business on their part just as it was business for me to mislead the spies. I rarely have been able to keep the same set of betting commissioners for any length of time, with the exception of Walter Keyes and my nephew, Jimmy McGill. A few bets and my commissioners were pointed out and watched. Some of the men I have used were most interesting. I have taken them from almost every walk of life.

It has happened many a time that a bookmaker, in looking over his sheet after a race, has found wagers of "fifties and hundreds," cash bets, and has wondered when a rural looking stranger has come to take down the winning. I have heard the bookmakers say to the cashier, looking at a long whiskered winner, "I wonder who that man is," to which the cashier replied, "He is a stranger to me." If that same bookmaker and cashier could have seen that rural-looking stranger later hand over to me the winnings, they would have regarded it as important knowledge. But I never told them; and sometimes, I never told my dearest friend, Walter Keyes, or my nephew. I have had strangers work for me for weeks before somebody discovered the trick, after which the man's usefulness was destroyed.

To conclude this chapter, the financing of your money is the high road to success. Learn when to put down a heavy wager by picking out an almost sure winner. In a race where three or four horses have a chance to win, the odds are much against you and the wager should be small. Otherwise, pass the race up.

I have lost as many as twenty-seven straight bets and gotten even—and become a winner on the next two races. The average bettor should always cut his wagers when running in a losing streak and press them when luck favors him. Doubling bets when losing is ruination to any person. The time to double is when you have the bookmakers' money in hand. If a bookmaker gets you hooked, try to wiggle off with as little loss as possible—but if you get a bookmaker hooked, set in your money. And if your judgment is good and you go at him cold blooded, betting on what appears to be certainties, you have a grand chance to win a small fortune.

4
HANDICAPPING

Many systems are employed to handicap horses. Some are successful while others are decidedly faulty. In my opinion, the old-fashioned way of handicapping by comparison is the best—which is to draw conclusions from a weight and class standpoint, time being a minor consideration. Since the official handicapper takes weights for a foundation for his work, why should a player of horses employ a different system?

After the official handicapper has allotted the weights to be carried in a race, it is then that the player is put to the test: It is his judgment against that of the official handicapper. If he can find a flaw in the official handicapper's work, he will probably find the winner of the race. The player has a great advantage over the official handicapper, because he has the opportunity of considering the present condition of a horse, whereas the handicapper must not let such a factor enter into his calculations.

When the official handicapper starts his work, he bases his calculations on the best performance of every entry, and to him all entries are supposed to be in their best possible physical condition. For instance, when Mr. Vosburgh, the Jockey Club's official handicapper, gets the entries for the Suburban and Brooklyn Handicaps in January, and the races are not run until June, there is no chance for him to consider anything but the bare facts of horse-against-horse. He judges horses on their past histories, and thus allots the weights they are to carry so that, in his opinion, the race will finish in a dead heat, as it were. In his calculation, he endeavors to weight each so that all will finish together.

However, condition enters so much into such races as the Brooklyn and Suburban Handicap that out of an entry of seventy or eighty horses, sometimes no more than ten go to the post. This is not always because the owners are unsatisfied with the weights allotted, but on account of sickness or mishaps of some kind that have come to the horses during their preparation, which prevents them from being sent to the post. It is rarely that more than fifteen per cent of the entries in the classical handicaps go to the post, and not more than from seven to ten per cent in the big stake races. This shows the value of the condition of a thoroughbred when called upon to race.

HORSES MUST BE IN
TOP CONDITION

It is a fact that the condition of a horse in a race has considerably more to do with his winning or losing than the weight he carries. In other words, a horse might be allotted 126 pounds in a handicap, and then he might be beaten by a moderate horse carrying only 110 pounds. This does not mean that the moderate horse will always beat him at that difference in weight, for the condition of the two horses might reverse matters very decidedly a week or two later. A horse usually carrying top weight in a handicap cannot win with 90 pounds up if he is not in condition. Sysonby once ran a dead heat with Race King. Such a result could not have been possible with both horses at their best.

For instance, a horse in the Brooklyn Handicap carrying 110 pounds might beat the top weight carrying 126 pounds, yet in the Suburban, the condition of the top weight would be so much improved that he would run away from the horse that beat him in the Brooklyn. If you review the records of the classical handicaps, you will see that such cases have frequently occurred. This demonstrates absolutely that the player of horses, if he is a close student of the disposition of a horse and its condition, can almost tell the official handicapper what horses should be prominent at the finish with average racing luck. This is because he knows which horses are in the best condition.

Horses are the same as human beings where condition is the test of superiority. If a first class prizefighter, foot runner or athlete of any kind is not in good physical condition, he can be defeated by an inferior man; whereas, if both are in the best condition possible, there would be no question which one would win. It is exactly the same with horses. Picking the winner of a race rests entirely upon the ability of a man to tell when a horse is in good condition and when he is not.

If one good horse is not at his best and there are inferior horses that are at their best, they will beat him in nine cases out of ten. Hence the condition of a horse is of much greater importance to a person who is playing the races than adhering to the cast iron rule of some persons who say that because this horse gave that horse fifteen pounds in actual weight and beat him, he should beat him again today. While he might do it, it is not a sure thing because the reverse condition of the two horses might change the result. Because of this, many people attribute the result of a race to crookedness when it is nothing more nor less than the good condition of one horse and the lack of condition of another. The trainer may not be at fault. He has possibly done the best he could and possibly believes his horse to be in excellent condition. But horses cannot talk. They cannot tell you when they are not feeling well, and they do not always give any outward sign, though they occasionally do.

I have had horses that I believed to be in the most perfect condition, yet they ran disappointing races. I have seen horses work for a race and the work has been so impressive to my mind that I have made very large wagers on them—yet two days later in the actual race, when they should have run up to their work, they have fallen far behind. Many times a very fast work before a race does more harm to a horse than good. From this a very common saying has arisen among the trainers: "I worked my horse this morning 1 1/4 miles in 2.06, and he looks as if he will win sure." The other trainer will reply: "You have just about made him run his race today." It has been proven true time after time, the fast work of two days prior having dulled his speed.

START WITH SCALE WEIGHT

To get down to actual handicapping, you begin with the old-fashioned scale weight, wherein it is prescribed that horses of certain ages shall give horses their junior so much weight at certain distances, and at different seasons of the year. This scale is the real foundation of handicapping. After a race in which these horses have met, the handicapper will decide for himself which horse is the best under the scale condition. And in future races, he will put on or take off weight as he deems fit to bring them together, or to make them run a dead heat as it were.

A man like Mr. Vosburgh, who has had years of experience and has the value of every horse that he has seen run at his fingertips, can so allot the weights that to the casual onlooker, it will be mystifying. I have seen handicaps of ten horses in a race where it was next to impossible to tell which would win out of the ten. This is where the man who is a judge of the condition of a horse and of his disposition has an advantage over those who have not acquired such knowledge. It may be that some of the horses will not run over the track prescribed, while others have performed creditably over it. Some horses will not carry their weight as well as others. Then again, jockeys will make a great difference in the running of horses. All these things have to be considered.

Every horse must be treated separately and his entire disposition analyzed. Some things will be found in his favor and others will be found against him. After drawing a conclusion as to the most probable winner, it is important that you draw a mind picture of how the race will be run, for there are many times some horses are aided considerably by the way a race is run, while others are killed off early in the race.

One thing can be depended upon positively: If there are two or three very fast horses in a race, one or two of them will quit before the end of the journey if the route is of reasonable length. In other words, they will race themselves into the ground, generally because their jockeys have no better sense than to be carried along with the early pace in a race. It is in such cases that an intelligent rider will sometimes win on the third- or fourth-best horse. This is where an intelligent jockey has a great value, for he profits by the mistakes of others. And lest I forget it to mention it in later paragraphs, you can say right here that seventy-five per cent of the inconsistency in horseracing, which is generally put down to criminality, is nothing more nor less than lack of intelligence on the part of the jockeys.

Many times a handicapper is deceived in horses through their poor showing in races. This usually is when horses are going back after having reached the keen edge of condition. Sharp, practical trainers will then run them three or four times, knowing that they are not at their best, with the intention of getting the handicapper to reduce their weight in races. Then there will be a lapse of time before such a horse is entered again, but he will appear on the list with possibly the same weight to carry as he did in his last race. Instead of being in poor condition, the rest he has had will have done him good and he will be in perfect condition. It is in such cases that killings are made.

Speaking of killings, many are attempted but few are accomplished. The reason so few killings are made is that, while one man has been conniving to make a killing with one horse, there are others that have been playing the same game. Frequently, three or four killings are attempted in the same race, when only one can be made. The others will be losers.

CLOSELY OBSERVE THE TOTE BOARD

If a player can, through close observation of the market, find out that three or four different horses are being heavily played, it is a good time to test his skill as a handicapper to decide which is the best horse of the number and speculate accordingly. But if he cannot determine for himself—exclusive of tips, stable information and the like—which is the best horse, it is best for him to watch the race without speculating.

By watching rather than speculating, he will not confine his attention to the one horse he is playing, but instead will divide it between all the horses concerned. Thus, he may see something during the running of the race that will stand him in good stead upon some future occasion when the same horses meet again, as they frequently do after a short interval.

THE BIGGEST WIN I EVER ATTEMPTED TO MAKE

I have made several big winnings during my career. The biggest I ever attempted was on Parvenue, but unfortunately I did not win one-fifth of the money that I should have won, owing to a technicality. I owned Parvenue and he was a good racehorse, so good that I never really knew how good he was. A race came up at Monmouth Park for which he was eligible and I prepared him for it. Prior to my purchase of him, Parvenue was a common sort of horse, but he improved much after I bought him; consequently few knew very much about him, or even entertained the thought of his improving sufficiently to beat good horses. But he had shown me in his work that he could do almost anything I wanted him to do. He looked to be such a good investment to me that I had five or six men in the poolrooms of New York, of which there were many in those days, and each one had from two thousand to four thousand dollars to invest.

When the betting opened, Parvenue was quoted in some books as high as forty to one, and my commissioners told me afterwards that they placed some money at those odds, and that the lowest price they took was fifteen to one. At the track I also had several commissioners betting my money, and the lowest they got was twelve to one.

Just before it was time to go to the post, there was some trouble in the steward's stand. A horse, I believe it was Dagonet, had been carded on the program to carry a certain weight when, according to the condition, he should have had a much lighter or heavier impost. The mistake was not discovered until nearly post time, and the stewards decided to scratch the horse. All bets were declared off, and a new book was made. This, of course, upset my calculations entirely. It at once disturbed the equilibrium of things. The men in the poolrooms who had bet my money had to wait in line to get their money back again, and when the new prices were put up, Parvenue was quoted at much less odds owing to the big commission having been placed all over town and becoming common property.

The same condition existed at the track: My commissioners there had to wait to get their money back before they could bet it again, and this time when the prices were quoted, the highest I got was twelve to one. Much of the money was placed back again on the horse by my commissioners in the city and on the track, but nothing like the original amounts.

It is unnecessary to say that Parvenue won all by himself. After all that trouble and excitement, I won over $45,000. I was so disgusted with the turn that affairs had taken that I really never reckoned up how much money I would have won on the race if the bets had not been declared off the first time, but it would have been an enormous sum.

A note from Edward W. Cole:

I interviewed Sam Doggett, who rode Parvenue in this celebrated race, and he gave me the most lucid description of Pittsburgh Phil's confidence in the horse and his coolness under such nerve-straining conditions. He had thousands upon thousands of dollars at stake when he gave Doggett instructions on how to ride. In the language of Doggett:

"Pittsburgh came into the paddock and said to me, 'Sam, you are riding a pretty good horse. Just let him rate along, and when you get to the head of the stretch, let him down for a few strides and you will be in front. After you get there, do not show him up too much.'

"If he had been my horse and I had four hundred dollars depending on him, I would have won by a sixteenth of a mile if I could. I think that if I had ever known the amount of money Pittsburgh stood to win on that horse, I do not really know what would have happened, but I did not know that he was betting more than one hundred dollars on him. You talk about a cool and collected man, Pittsburgh Phil stood alone. He knew more about horses and horse racing than anyone and seemed to have phenomenal knowledge and confidence in his own ability."

SPECULATING ON HANDICAP RACES

In handicaps, the top weights are always at a disadvantage unless they are very high-class horses, for the reason that they have to do so much more work than their opponents. It is not advisable for the top weights in a long race, say at one and a quarter miles or longer, either to make the pace or follow it too closely; for if there is too much speed in the early stages of the race, it will affect the horses that try to keep up with the leaders. Hence, you will notice that the top weights are generally mixed up in the middle of the bunch, or in the rear if they happen to get off badly, which causes them effort in threading their way through the field, especially if it contains anywhere from twelve to sixteen horses.

They have to be very intelligently ridden to avoid interferences from horses that are dropping back. Many times, they have to run outside three or four horses when they are making their run, which is very costly, because a horse loses considerable ground in running outside other horses. Then there is always the chance of their being jumped on or cut down in a race. In fact, there is so much racing luck against horses, especially those carrying the heavier weights, that they are many times beaten through bad luck.

I once went over the year's record of Ethelbert and found that he had lost thirty per cent of his races through bad racing luck—races that he would have won under normal conditions. This rule would not apply to a horse like Hamburg or any very high-class horse, because a real high-class horse is good enough to go to the front from the start; or attain such a position in the advance guard that he will not be bothered nearly so much as a horse like Ethelbert, which was not a high-class horse but merely a first-class handicap horse.

All these things have to be considered well when seeking the winner of a handicap, or in fact any other kind of race. Many a time a good horse is beaten in the spring of the year through lack of condition. There are few trainers who can send a horse to the post the first time out for a big race in perfect condition. The horse may appear so to them, but they lose sight of the fact that a horse that has been trained for the race in private should be fit to run a mile and a quarter if he is expected to run a mile race. I mean by this that when a horse has not had a race for some months and has been prepared for a hard struggle, he loses a certain amount of nervous energy while walking round the paddock, while being saddled, while in the parade going to the post, and while waiting for a start.

THE TEMPERAMENT OF THE HORSE

Horses are high strung and of nervous temperament. They waste a whole lot of energy—and a great deal more the first time out after a let up—than they do after a race or two. There is nothing like racing horses to be assured of their condition. One race for a horse is equal to two or three private trials. It will do him more good, it will make him hardier, and it will relieve his nervous condition considerably.

A horse can be compared to an actor in this regard. An actor going to produce a new play, while he has all the ability and is satisfied in himself that he is perfect in every detail, will invariably falter at some stage or another the first night; but he will improve after that first night's experience. So it is with the majority of horses. There are some horses that seem to be devoid of nervousness. They do not fret or worry about anything. McChesney is an example. There was a horse that walked around the paddock like an old cow. He would not lose an ounce of nervous energy in a year under any condition. If he were keyed up to run one mile and a quarter, he would run one mile and a quarter. You could bet anything that he would run the race that he was ready for. McChesney is an exception in this regard.

It is in such cases as these that the "clocker," the man who gets up at three o'clock in the morning to watch the horses working, is a necessary adjunct to a successful horse player. If he is a good man, he will tell you exactly what the horses are doing and how they are doing it. It is not always a question with him that because a horse has worked three-quarters in 1.13, he should beat a horse that has only worked three quarters in 1.14. The horse that has worked in 1.13 has possibly received a hurried preparation and, being of a nervous disposition, possibly would lose a certain amount of energy before a race, while the horse that has been worked in 1.14 has been steadily prepared and possibly carried heavier weights while working than the horse that worked in 1.13.

It does not follow that because a horse has worked three-quarters in 1.13 that he will run in 1.13 in his race. He may do it much better alone than in company. It is in such cases that the disposition of a horse is the deciding factor. Then again, a horse may be fully extended that has worked in 1.13, while the horse that worked in 1.14 had considerable in reserve. It is only the expert "clocker" who can discover such things by his constant watchfulness.

TRACK CONDITIONS ARE IMPORTANT

I have found that track conditions are of the utmost importance, and the surroundings of a racetrack have a great effect on some horses. Some horses will run good races over certain tracks, while in the same company and under similar conditions on other tracks, they will run very disappointingly. A horse will run a good race at Sheepshead Bay while at Gravesend he will run quite the contrary.

There also are horses that like the shape of some tracks and not others, but I attribute this change of form to the action of a horse more than anything else. There are many horses that cannot make sharp turns, while others are exceedingly nimble. For instance, Lady Amelia can run around a hat, while a great big horse finds it difficult to make a good turn. Hermis can run on any old track. He is a good horse. The same can be said of Beldame. In fact, good levelheaded thoroughbreds can be depended upon almost anywhere. It is only what I term "sucker" horses that have likes and dislikes.

The Bennings track, for instance, has a very deep soil, and it takes a mighty muscular horse to win there. It needs a horse with strength. A strong horse with only moderate speed—a rater I might say—would beat a much faster horse at Bennings because the fast horse would become leg weary, and the strong horse will get him when he is nearing the finish. On any track like Bennings where the going is deep and of a sandy nature, it is a good system to play horses that have shown a liking for such a track. If you will look over the records, you will find that winners repeat frequently, while those that are defeated will be defeated almost continuously.

I have won many wagers through studying the disposition of horses on certain tracks. Nothing could be more noticeable in this respect than the running of some horses on the grass track at Sheepshead Bay. It is a recognized fact that some horses improve many pounds over the grass course. One in particular, Decanter, you could always depend upon to run a good race over the turf.

There is another important item in regard to the turf course at Sheepshead Bay: It has a peculiar formation, and one of the fundamental principles in trying to figure out the winner is the early speed of a horse. Early speed is essential and a horse possessing that commodity has a much better chance to win over the turf course at Sheepshead Bay than a slow beginner, as the trailing horses usually go very wide on the turns owing to their not being banked the same as they are on the main courses. While horses do win over the turf course and come from rear positions, they have to be much the best.

Another fact that I discovered in horses racing over the turf is that they will go further than they will over a dirt course. They do not get tired so quickly. A sprinter, which has been used to running three-quarters of a mile, will go a mile over the turf invariably. A horse accustomed to running one and one-sixteenth-mile races will hold out for one mile and a quarter on the turf. I was never satisfied as to the cause of this, but thought possibly that the footing was better and did not cup out with the horses like it does over a dirt course, which is naturally trying on the muscles, as it is to a man who tries to run over the sand at the seashore.

5

THE FALLACY OF HANDICAPPING BY TIME

Quite a number of systematic handicappers take time as a basis for their calculations. I could never see where time was a positive criterion. Time enters into the argument under certain conditions, but if depended upon entirely for a deduction, it will be found wanting. The atmospheric conditions will have much to do with the time of a race, and the way a race is run will also have much to do with the time of such race.

Here is a positive illustration of this: The match race between Admiration and May Hempstead at Sheepshead Bay was run in 1.40 1-5. Some days before the match race, both fillies ran in two different races at a mile, with Admiration carrying 111 lbs. and May Hempstead 107 lbs. Admiration ran in 1.41 and May Hempstead in 1.39 1-5. Making allowance for weight, those who handicapped the match race by time might expect both horses to run under 1.40 when they met in their duel.

What was the result? Admiration won the match race in 1.40 1-5. May Hempstead was beaten by many lengths, yet she had covered the same course in 1.39 1-5 under almost identical conditions, even as regards the atmosphere. The cause of this change in time was due entirely to the way the match race was run. It was the early pace that made the time slow, the first half mile being run in something less than 47 seconds, and it became a question of sheer gameness as to which mare would crack first. One of them had to wilt under the terrific pace, as is always the case in races where two or more horses are being driven to their limit of speed in the early part of the race. No better illustration of the uncertainty of time as a basis for handicapping could be given than the Admiration and May Hempstead races.

Again, it will frequently be found on record that a horse running in his own class, say a race for three-year-olds only, carrying 112 pounds will run three-quarters of a mile in 1.13, and possibly win with apparent ease. This same horse will come out three or four days later in a race for horses three years old and upward, meet a horse like Hermis or Voter (in fact, any fast horse), and possibly he will carry but 95 pounds. A time handicapper would possibly make the three-year-old run in 1.12 if he carried out his calculations to a fraction. What would be the result of the race? Hermis would beat such a horse in a gallop, and possibly would not have to run but six furlongs better than 1.14 to do it. Class accounts for this result. Being a high-class horse, Hermis would take a three-year-old by the collar and he would run him into the ground in the first half mile, leaving him so leg weary at the end of this distance that he would simply stagger home. In such cases, time is absolutely useless and deceiving.

AN EXCEPTION TO THE FALLACY

There are instances, however, where it is possible to determine a good race from a bad race by time when two races are run on the same day. Time again is useful to the trainer who is watching for improvement in his horse, but it is not nearly as reliable in a trial as running one horse against another. For instance, I may have a maiden in my stable that cannot work a mile better than 1.45, yet if I start him off with Belmar for a mile trial, he will run a mile in 1.41 or perhaps better. Such a horse is considered a poor workhorse, one that will race much better than he works. On the other hand, there are horses that will work exceedingly fast when alone and will not run up to form in races. Such horses are very bad betting propositions.

Returning to the fallacy of time as a criterion of what horses should do and should not do, there are horses that have created records on many occasions that have never lived up to their record afterward or anywhere near it. Take a straight course, for instance, like the Futurity Course in Sheepshead Bay. Time is of absolutely no use there, because there may be a wind playing down the chute that is almost a gale, and it will cause the time of the race to be exceedingly fast. Or the wind may be playing head on, which would make the time of the race very slow since the resistance of the wind is very great in a horserace; of course, it is correspondingly great when acting as a propeller.

There are no race-going folks who can determine the velocity of the wind. Similar results follow, though probably not so decided, on a circular course as on a straight stretch. The wind sometimes blows across the track; sometimes it aids the horses on the backstretch; or it may be against them coming home. Then again, it may be against them on the backstretch and aid them coming home. A horse can run faster against the wind in the early stages of the race than he can when he becomes leg weary in the last quarter of a mile. Then there is the sultry day with a great deal of humidity, as well as the hot bright day when the atmosphere is dry. All these things have an effect on the time of the race and, in fact, on the condition of a horse. It is a common saying that such-and-such a horse is a "hot weather horse," and that others will be better in the hot weather. Weather affects them as it does persons.

It is almost unnecessary to go further into the details on the question of time as a handicapping basis, for I have given enough illustrations of the uncertainty of making time the foundation or basic calculation in handicapping. Horse against horse, weight against weight, and accompanying conditions are the best lines to follow as to the superiority of one horse over another.

DO NOT OVERVALUE
YOUR OPINIONS

Some men will say that because a horse has run a mile in 1.40 one day and was beaten in 1.41 the next, that there was something crooked about the horse. Do not believe it. I am not saying that there is no crookedness in horse racing. There is crookedness, more or less, in every kind of business, at least in most kinds of business. The less one thinks of crookedness in horse racing the better will it be for him. There are some smart men—that is, men who consider themselves smart because they cook up a race once in a while—but if you will look them over, you will find that they possess money spasmodically and generally wind up their careers poor.

Instead of looking for crookedness in a race, be conservative and try to find out, after study of the race, where it was possible to show a defect in your own calculations instead of jumping at the conclusion that because a horse did not run directly up to your own deductions, the race was crooked. If you will place more confidence in the result of the race than you do in an exalted opinion of your own handicapping, you will find that you will be much better off and considerably richer in the end.

When I play a horse in a race and he is beaten on his merits, I know that I have made a mistake somewhere in my deductions. Before I go to sleep that night I try to find out where that mistake is, and turn it to advantage in the future. If everybody who depends upon his own opinion in speculating on horses will follow this advice, he will find it very instructive, and in the end much more profitable than jumping at the conclusion that there was something crooked about the race.

6
HANDICAPPING BY CLASS AND WEIGHT

Class and weight are two of the most important subjects to be considered under the general division of handicapping. Although class is not so closely related to the actual mechanical work of bookkeeping as weight, it cannot be overlooked. When it comes to handicapping, all your mechanical work will go for naught if you have no knowledge of class.

"Show me the man who can class horses correctly and I will show you the man who can win all the money he wants—and he only needs a dollar to start."

Mike Dwyer said that to me years ago, and time has shown it to be one of the greatest truths ever uttered about horseracing. Class, that intangible thing that almost defies definition, controls almost positively the running of thoroughbreds! Class enables one horse to beat another no matter what the physical odds imposed may be, what the conditions are or what the distance is. You may say it is that which enables a light bull terrier to whip a big dog of another breed. It enables one fighter to whip another. As I said before, it is hard to define, but everybody discerns it when it is there.

In trying to define class in horse racing, the best I can do is to say that class in a horse is the ability possessed by it to carry its stipulated stake weight, take the track, and go the distance that nature intended it to go. It is heart, nerve and ability combined, which ignores all ordinary rules and ordinary obstacles.

There is no law by which you determine class or classify horses. An intimate knowledge of a horse alone tells—what he has done and how he has done it places him, and nothing else. Birth and breeding do not appear to count so much. Many great stallions, themselves of high class and with great turf records, have never sired good horses, not even when the nick has been with mares of equally high class. On the other hand, stallions that have not been so great have produced magnificent colts; and it is the same way with the mares.

One of the mysterious rules of class that I cannot understand is that a real high-class horse and a positively common horse cannot be brought together by weights within the handicapper's reason. You could put 140 pounds on Hamburg, a really high-class horse, and 80 pounds on Alsike, and Hamburg would run him into the ground. He could take the track and outrun Alsike at every stage—and the weight would not make any difference. You have seen what Reliable, a high-class sprinter, has done and what Kinley Mack, Gold Heels, Ethelbert, and all high-class horses can do.

CLASSIFYING HORSES

Out of all the horses foaled during the year, there is hardly one-tenth of one percent that can be termed positively high class. After that stage comes the first-class handicap horse and the proportion grows larger; then follows the moderate handicap horse, still more; then comes the lowest form of handicap horses, which dovetail into the selling "plater" class of the first flight. And from there they grade down to the "dogs," the poorest horses running.

Now, between the really high-class horse like Hamburg and the "dog" like Alsike, there is such a wide gulf that the blindest man on the track can detect it. If that were all there is to it, racing would be easy. But then you start to go down from the top and come up from the bottom and your trouble begins. Between the first-class handicap horses and the horses a notch above the "dogs," you have not so much trouble. After that, it grows harder until finally the classes dovetail, and then only the shrewdest of observers can hope to make a successful classification. As there are more horses in the dovetailing classes than anywhere else, there are more races in those divisions, and hence one of the great uncertainties of racing. But the mysterious rule applies just the same—the better class horse has a "shade" always on the one below him—but very often, we cannot fathom it.

Right here I may say that I consider Gold Heels a real high-class horse, for he did in the Brighton handicap what only such horses can do. During the running of that race he stood off three challenges, one horse after another coming up to him in an effort to get the track away from him. You will remember how he stood them off one by one, taking them by the neck and beating them until Blues came up. Blues he beat from the eighth pole home in one of the greatest struggles we have ever seen on the racetrack. Gold Heels is to me a grand racehorse.

By observation, class can be detected and tabulated in horses of a lower grade. For instance, there are many horses that will run an exceedingly good race with 90 pounds up, while 103 or 104 pounds will cause them to make a very disappointing showing. Every pound seems to send them down the scale of class. Knowledge of this fact is very valuable to you.

It is this class that is most frequently manipulated by trainers and owners. Entered, say, at 108 pounds, this kind of a horse will show nothing. There will be two or three races just like it until the general public will classify that particular horse as a hound. Then will come a race in which the impost will be 95 pounds. The public, which does not study or observe closely, will pass him over again. They will not have noticed that his races with heavier weights have improved the horse, that he is fit, and that everything is propitious. He improves alarmingly, and immediately a cry goes up. Strictly speaking, there was no cheating by those concerned in the horse. He ran as far as he could with 108 pounds up in his prior races, but nature had not made him a 108-pound horse.

You will find this kind of horse in the moderate and fairly good class of horses. For instance, there was Imp. She could always be depended upon to do the best she could under any and all conditions. With 112 pounds on her, she could beat first-class horses at a mile and a quarter, but every pound more than that would send her down the scale. With 118 pounds, she could beat high-class horses for one and one-eighth miles, but if asked to go one and one-quarter miles with the same weight, she would die away in the last furlong. She could carry 121 pounds one mile and a sixteenth and beat good horses, but after that distance the weight would be fatal. I use Imp as an example: There are many of a similar disposition and class in her division, running every year.

THE IMPORTANCE OF WEIGHT

In regard to horses carrying weight, I figure that two-year-olds can give considerably more weight away successfully than horses in other divisions. A true high-class two-year-old will carry a lot of weight, and it is hard to stop him until he is asked to carry 130 pounds or more (and sometimes not even then). In my experience, I have found that a high-class two-year-old with 130 pounds on him will race practically as fast as he can with 120 pounds on him. In saying this, I merely infer that the difference in a race that a horse will run is so slight that it is hardly discernible. This refers to real first-class two-year-olds.

In the lower division of two-year-olds, a few pounds make a very material difference to their racing. In fact, a difference of five pounds, say from 100 to 105 pounds on a common horse, will make him run a very inferior race. And when a common horse is asked to carry 112 pounds or 115 pounds, it seems to take his speed away altogether. Go back over any records of high-class two-year-olds and you will find that this assertion is absolutely correct. Hamburg was an extraordinary weight carrying two-year-old, and he is only one of many that could be mentioned.

A good trainer will know just about what weight his horse can carry and run a good race. He knows that if his horse is at his best with 95 pounds up, he will run a very bad race if he puts 107 pounds on him. Frequently a trainer will enter a cheap selling plater in a race with the selling price so high that the horse will have to carry 110 pounds or thereabouts. He knows at the time that his horse will run poorly and has probably entered him for work only, preparing him for a race in the very near future when he will be entered to carry 95 pounds.

These little tricks are well worth watching, for by close observation you can easily see what a trainer is doing with his horses and what his intentions are. In other words, when you have so far discovered the weight carrying ability of a horse, and you see him in a race with considerably more weight up than in your opinion he can carry, it is safe to say that this horse can be thrown into the discard. Then you can depend on the old adage, "Watch and wait." Do not understand me as saying that all trainers resort to these tricks. The majority do not; this is a point that the player of horses has to learn. He must study the disposition of the men who train horses, as well as the horses themselves.

I have found that, everything being equal, two-year-olds run much more consistently than any other class of horses. They are taught to race. They are young and they know nothing else. In fact, they are just like children playing on tiptoe all the time. Their consistency is due to their inexperience, for with age comes cunning and the development of a disposition that is either good or bad. Some horses retain an even disposition throughout their career, while others become exceedingly eccentric. It is a common expression on the turf that a horse is "getting cunning," which means that if things suit him, he will run a good race; but if they do not suit him, he will perform very indifferently. Good horses have a lot of character about them, and they will run very consistently when in first class condition. A horse that has become eccentric in his disposition is liable to perform very indifferently. There are hundreds of horses that can win and will not run their best—horses that will work alone in the morning and shirk in the afternoon.

THE USE OF STIMULANTS

Administering stimulants to horses came about due to the fact that some could run but would not. In these days, they are called "dope" horses because they are stimulated with drugs. Before the stimulating drug was discovered, a draft of sherry or whiskey mixed with coffee was given to horses in the shape of a drench. It has been known to have effect, but progress and experiments afterward proved that drugs were absolutely essential to make some horses put forth their best efforts. The drug question has been a very serious proposition for years, and at one time was beyond the control of racing officials. It is even now a source of considerable trouble. When the use of stimulants became prevalent, I carefully studied the question, frequently getting advice from veterinary surgeons as to the effect that certain kinds of drugs would have on horses. It was an exceedingly vexing question with me, for on that problem alone depended many of my investments.

When I discovered that a horse was a "dope" horse, it was absolutely necessary for me to know whether a stimulant had been given to him or not. I needed this information for two reasons:

1. In my investigation, if I found that the horse had been given a stimulant, I knew he should run a good race, and therefore become a factor in my calculations;

2. On the contrary, if he had not been stimulated by drugs, it was equivalent to his not being in the race at all. If the horse in mind was one of the choices, it was a safe betting proposition to bet against him, and look elsewhere for the winner.

It was sometimes very easy to beat a race two ways under such conditions, and I have frequently played the winner of a race and laid against another.

It is rather difficult these days to tell when horses have been drugged, for different drugs have different effects on horses. In the old days, it was generally conceded that if a horse "broke out" into a pronounced perspiration, he was drugged. In my experience, sometimes he was and sometimes not. The fretful horse will "break out" any day while in the paddock, and nearly all horses will show some perspiration on a hot day, so that if any of them have been drugged, it cannot always be detected by their coat. But there are two things that hardly ever fail in distinguishing a horse that has been stimulated and a horse that has not. The first is the glassy appearance of the eye and its bright, anxious look. The pupil also dilates. The second sign is the nostril, which becomes considerably distended. The breathing also is not uniform. The nostrils will expand and contract in an unusual manner. In some instances, the forehead and the hide around the top of the head and neck will show continued perspiration.

Those who have used stimulants on horses have things down pretty fine. They cannot stop the look in the eyes and the distending of the nostrils, but they can make their horses look as if they had been doped when such is not the case. Giving them a good stiff preliminary breeze under very heavy blankets will cause horses to have a doped appearance. In many cases, this avoids suspicion and eludes the vigilance of the racing officials after they are drugged, because the horse goes to the post in apparently the same condition as regards his outward appearance every time. If it were possible to make owners and trainers send their horses to the post in the same condition at all times, stimulating horses would not create the scandal that it does, for the horses would run consistently.

It is the abuse of stimulants that causes so much criticism—using them one day and not another. This abuse creates scandal and denunciation of the sport. All the patrons of racing want is consistency in horses; and when it is possible, they should get it. There is enough natural inconsistency in horse racing without its being forced upon the public by unscrupulous men.

7
THE TREATMENT
OF HORSES

Many owners and trainers make mistakes and frequently spoil a good horse by not making him happy in his surroundings. A horse is just like a person in this respect. To do his best work, he must be contented. Whenever I bought a horse, my first object was to find out his disposition. I have watched him closely in his stall, watched his eating, whether he had a good appetite or minced at his meals. Any failing he had I would always try to remedy in some way or another. A horse that is not contented in his stable cannot take on flesh or be happy. Horses will not permit certain stable hands around them and they will even shirk their meals if interrupted by someone they do not like.

Belmar was a horse that was very hard to please. I knew he was a very good horse, but I also knew that there was something wrong with him. He never seemed to run the race that I believed he could run. I bought this horse from Mr. Galway, thinking I could manage him and bring out his best qualities. Almost every moment I had to spare I would spend around Belmar's stall. I told my brother, William, that if ever we could get at the horse's disposition, he would win a lot of races. We tried to please him by putting a companion in his stall in the shape of a rooster. He did not seem to take to the rooster, so we tried a cat and a goat. Finally, a little fox terrier playing around the stables ran into the stall and Belmar seemed to take to him at once.

After that, if the fox terrier were away from Belmar, the old horse would sulk and whinny for him to come back again. When Belmar was lying down, the little old fox terrier was always lying on his shoulder and the two always slept together. It got so that the fox terrier could be placed on the withers of Belmar and he would trot around the shed with the dog on his back.

No sooner had Belmar become contented with his surroundings that he began to run good races. If I remember rightly, Mr. Vosburgh, unquestionably one of the few high-class handicappers that this or any other country has ever seen, had Belmar handicapped at 95 pounds in races before I got him. So much did the horse improve that he won seven straight handicaps without being defeated—and each time his weight was increased until in the last of his winning series, he carried 128 pounds. In other words, he had jumped from the bottom to the top of the ladder in the handicap division, and it was all due to his being made happy and contented in his surroundings.

There was always something very noticeable about Belmar at this time: his excellent condition after a race. It was very rare to see him pulling up distressed, and it is for this reason that I am egotistic enough to say that I improved Belmar faster than the handicapper put on weight. I never bought but one horse in my life that did not win any races for me. I can safely say that every horse I ever owned improved after I had him long enough to study his disposition.

A HORSE MUST FEEL COMFORTABLE

A horse should be made comfortable at all times. There is no animal so near like a person in disposition as a horse. They are positively human in their conduct at times. A trainer should use his best efforts to control a horse with a nervous disposition, for it is exceedingly hard to make them take on flesh and do well. The mind of a horse should be easy—he should not be anticipating anything, he should not be teased or in any way abused. Like a person, if irritable or excitable, a horse loses flesh and is incapable of his best efforts.

It sometimes takes months to get at the true disposition of a horse. Exceedingly close watch must be kept on him and every effort made to make him understand what is wanted of him. When a horse is fit to race, it is almost cruel not to race him at least once a week. A horse expects to race if he is a thoroughbred. It is his nature, and if he is not raced he is disappointed and fretful. This is very logical and has its resemblance in the eagerness a gamecock shows to fight. There is no time that a gamecock is not ready to get into a scrap if he is fit. It is the same with a thoroughbred: He is high-strung and must be raced. Moreover, while in this condition he will improve with racing and the work keeps him from being fretful, which is the main point in keeping a horse up to his condition.

This does not mean, however, that a horse will keep on improving after a certain time. When he has reached the keen edge of condition, he will begin to go back. An oarsman or a pugilist, or any other human being who has been keyed up to the top notch by continued effort, will go stale. That also happens to a horse. Therefore, the critical eye of the trainer should detect when to let up on a horse and not expect to keep him in first-class condition forever.

There is one instance that I can recall in particular. It was at Brighton Beach, where the condition of a horse after a race was so palpable to me that it made me win one of the biggest bets of the year. It was the race in which the horses Proper and Rigodon ran. Proper beat Rigodon, but in watching the horses return to the judges, as I always did, I saw that Proper was very much distressed while Rigodon did not appear to be in the least exhausted. He just took a couple of long breaths, then pricked up his ears and looked up and down the stretch as unconcerned as if he had not been in a race at all.

Shortly after this occurrence the same two horses ran again. My observations had shown me that Proper would not run as good a race the second time, owing to his being so much distressed after his prior racing. On the other hand, Rigodon would improve considerably. I naturally had quite a large wager on Rigodon and he won very handily.

It looked like a serious change of form, and so it was. There was considerable newspaper criticism about the two races: Quite a number of very smart men could not understand why Proper should beat Rigodon so handily one day and be so badly beaten by the same horse a few days later. In my opinion, it was nothing else in the world but a case of Rigodon improving and Proper having gone backward. In other words, the first race improved one horse considerably while it had a very distressing effect on the other.

8
WILLIAM COWAN ON PITTSBURGH PHIL

William Cowan, one of the very few expert bookmakers of this country, tells many incidents in the life of Pittsburgh Phil which prove the latter's close observation of the surroundings of a racetrack, the actions of men, and the unscrupulous ways some of them have of getting money at the expense of others. The following are his comments.

"It was always a battle between Phil and the bookmakers," said Cowan. "There was no time when he was interested in a race that he did not come pretty nearly knowing what was going on in every quarter of the ring. His scouts would report to him every minute, and he would weave the reports together until he came to a satisfactory conclusion of what to expect in the race.

"I made considerable money through Phil by closely watching his work. My partners have said to me many a time that it was hard business to deal with Phil. So it was, but being strictly a percentage bookmaker, I could make money from him just as I could from anyone else. I used to tell Phil that I gathered up a heap of money from the smaller players and then he would come along with a pushcart and take it away in a lump.

"But I always kept some of it, which was satisfying to me. For instance, if I could take $10,000 off horses that I knew he was not going to bet on, I could afford to give him a good bet at a fair average price on the horse he wanted.

"From his conversation, I would try to figure out what he was doing at all times, as he usually came to me first to get a line on the market. Many a time he has offered me a bet of $500 on a horse that I knew was only a stall. I would say, 'Come on, dump in what you want to bet.' He would laugh and reply, 'Well, make it $1,000.' He threw that money away to make me believe he was not stalling, as they say in turf vernacular. Twice he did that to me, and the next time he came along offering me $500. I suggested that he give me all the commission, believing that he was still stalling. He asked me how much I would take on the horse and I replied, '$1,000 across the board." And he dropped it in on me. I think the odds were six, two and even. He hooked me good. You see, he had thrown $1,500 away in prior bets knowing that I knew he was only stalling. Then he came along with the right one and took me for $9,000! We had many a laugh about it afterwards.

BETTING ON CINCINNATUS

"I remember one day at Brighton Beach when he came up to me and bet $400 straight, $600 place, and $1,000 third on Cincinnatus. I asked him if he wanted any more but he declined. As usual, there was a big crowd following him, all eager to listen to our conversation. For the benefit of the crowd, he said, 'I don't think he has much chance to win but he may stagger into the money. That's the reason I bet the $1,000 on him to show, to save the straight and place money.' He knew that if he made me a big bet of $1,000 or $2,000 straight, the

WILLIAM COWAN ON PITTSBURGH PHIL

bookmakers' runners would circulate it all over the ring in a minute and he would get no price. I believed he was sincere about the horse and kept his winning and place price up at 12 to 1 straight and 5 to 1 place, cutting only the third quotations.

"As many of the smaller bookmakers took their prices from my slate, the odds were held at my figures all over the ring. Every now and then, a bet of $100 cash money would be handed to me and I was willing to take it relying on Phil's word that he thought Cincinnatus might struggle home in third place. How many of these hundred-dollar bets were placed nobody will ever know, but there were scores of them, and they were bet by strangers. Toward the close of the betting, there was a whole lot of $100 bills for Cincinnatus. Every bookmaker was loaded up.

"It is little use relating the result of the race. If you remember, Cincinnatus won by something like a dozen lengths. Phil never told me how much he won, but it was a terrific bundle. Afterwards, he explained to me that his reason for not betting me more than $400 straight and $600 place was that I should keep the price up for his commissioners, who had orders to begin betting at a certain time. All those one-hundred-dollar bills that were bet on Cincinnatus in the late market belonged to Phil! Had he loaded me up with $1,000 across the board, he would have taken a very short price for the remainder of his commission. As it was, he averaged something like 10 to 1 for several thousands of dollars.

PITTSBURGH PHIL, DETECTIVE

"Another instance of his knowledge of the ring and its connections is amusing. He was being 'torched,' as the saying goes, which means that one or more of his employees would give out advance information to two or three bookmakers. These commissioners would tip the bookmakers as to their instructions,

and their business would be to send out big sums to bet on the horse Phil was going to play, thereby getting the top price.

"For instance, they would possibly get 5 to 1 against a horse through the advance information, and when Phil's commissioners would come around, they would sell it to them at 3 to 1, since any horse Phil played would invariably drop several points in the market. Phil watched the market closely for a while and finally discovered the leak. Then he set up a job and discovered everybody concerned. He called the commissioners to him whom he suspected, and gave them instructions to bet an unlimited amount on a horse that was quoted at 6 to 1. 'I don't want you to stop betting until that horse is 3 to 1 all over the ring,' he told them

"As anticipated by Phil, the order had no sooner been issued than the committee met, meaning the commissioners and the bookmakers, and the bookmakers at once sent out several thousand dollars to get 6 to 1. But after Phil's commissioners had tipped off the bookmakers, Phil called his men in and told them to wait a minute or two before beginning operations. He did this to give the bookmakers who were doing business with the commissioners enough time to put in their money, which they did. And without a cent of Phil's money going into the ring, the horse was knocked down to 4 to 1 in less time than it takes to tell it. This was convincing proof that these certain commissioners had been torching him. He was his own detective and he was the means of making three conniving bookmakers lose more money than they had made by subsidizing his commissioners.

"It is safe to say that never was there a man on the turf in any country who made such a study of it as Pittsburgh Phil. He threw every angle and turn from the racehorse down to the runner for a book. I have paid him more money than any twenty men who have done business with me. As I said before, I used to collect in bits and he would come along with a pushcart and take it away in a lump."

9
HOW PITTSBURGH PHIL
GAVE TOD SLOAN HIS START

BY WHICH THE JOCKEY AFTERWARD BECAME
FAMOUS IN THE TURF WORLD

Many stories have been written as to how Tod Sloan became famous as a jockey, and many have been told as to who it was that gave him his first opportunity. Sloan had been riding horses for a long period before he was heralded as one of the most famous horsemen in turf history. All reports to the contrary, it was Pittsburgh Phil who gave him his real start and it was an upright beginning.

It was in the late nineties that Pittsburgh Phil happened to be in California while racing was being conducted at the old Bay District track. It was a prolonged meeting and for some cause, which Phil attributed to a few of the conniving elements then rampant, he found himself a loser on the meeting to the extent of about $50,000. He had made up his mind to quit speculation, knowing that he could not succeed when there was so much in and out running, and where inconsistency in the handling of horses predominated.

He was inclined to believe that several of the jockeys were pulling horses in the interests of their employers. Many times one owner did not know what his neighbor was doing, and inconsistency was so pronounced that sometimes, three and four horses in a race were being taken care of by their riders; therefore, a horse would win that should have finished out of the money. The racing was so mystifying that a cold, deliberating handicapper, who depended upon form for his deductions, was a victim at almost every turn.

While Phil was sitting alone in the grandstand the day before he had decided to leave, Sloan, having no engagements to ride that day, happened to be not far away. When he noticed Phil in solitude, he went over and sat beside him. In those days, Sloan was hustling his way through the world as best he could, putting a bet down for himself when he had the money; and when he was without, doing his best to get someone to make a wager for him.

When Sloan was seated, he began a conversation: "I think such-and-such horse will win this race sure," said he to Phil, naming the horse to which he referred.

"What makes you think so, Tod?" returned Phil. "You rode him the last time he started and he finished way back." Phil knew what Sloan was driving at and was gathering such information from him as he could. "If he could not beat the lot that he met a few days ago, he cannot beat the field that he meets today."

"Well," said Sloan, "I'd like you to put a bet on him for me. He's as good as 7 to 1 in the betting. He'll win sure, Mr. Smith."

"Don't talk nonsense," returned Phil. "Why didn't he win the other day? Tell me why you think he can win today?" Though Phil asked these questions, he knew what the trouble had been in the previous race and merely wanted to learn what information Sloan would give.

"That horse was short the last time out," was all that Sloan said in answer to Phil's direct question.

"Well, I'm not going to bet any more on the races here," said Phil, "so I don't care to put a bet down for you, but sit here and we'll watch the race and if this horse wins, I will make you a proposition."

They sat together while the race was being run, and just as Sloan predicted, the horse won in a common gallop.

"Didn't I tell you he would win?" was Sloan's first remark after the horses had passed the winning post. "He was a good horse the other day but he met with a lot of interference, as well as being short of work."

"Say, Tod, why don't you make up your mind to be thorough in your work," asked Phil, "and ride from the drop of the hat? You'll make plenty of money and be successful. I will give you a start. I'll make an agreement with you if you will abide by it strictly and confidentially."

"What will you do?" asked Sloan.

"What will I do?" returned Phil, repeating the question while he gave himself time to think. "Why, I'll give you $400 every time you ride a winner at this track. It will make no difference whether I bet on it or not. If you win a race, you can go to my representative every Saturday night at the Palace Hotel and collect $400 for every winning mount you have had during the week. That's more money than you can make mixing up with sharps. And you will get your money—there will be no standing you up for it and paying off in promises. It will be in good, solid gold coin.

"There is one thing I shall want you to observe and that is secrecy. Upon no consideration must this interview be mentioned or even intimated. I do not wish to see you or be recognized by you. The only two things that you have to think about are winning a race and collecting $400 for so doing. If you win ten races next week, you can go direct to my representative and he will have instructions to pay you $4,000. Do not let your valet or anyone else know that you and I have had this conversation or that we have made an agreement."

"I'll do it!" Sloan decided. "I'll put all I know into every race that I ride. You can bet on me every time."

"Oh no," replied Phil, "I am not going to bet on you every time you ride, but I am going to bet when I think you are riding the best horse. But that will not make any difference in the fee part of the proposition. You will get your $400 if you win, whether I bet or not."

"It's a bargain. When does it begin?" asked Sloan.

"Tomorrow. And next Saturday, if you have ridden any winners, go to Mr. X (Phil was always discreet about letting the world know who was working for him and though he gave Sloan the name of his representative, he did not divulge it to me when telling the story) "and collect whatever money is coming to you. He will have full instructions to pay, no matter what the amount."

Only a person with turf wisdom such as Phil possessed could see his way clear to make such a proposition payable. But Phil knew what it meant to have a jockey trying to win every race against a half a dozen who were manipulating horses at the dictation of unscrupulous owners and trainers. Presumably, there were many times that Tod would win races through such manipulations, being "shooed in" as it were, and there was no question that some of his winning mounts would be quoted at ridiculous prices by the bookmakers. All these things had been well thought out by Phil and he laid his plans accordingly.

To keep the matter as quiet as possible, he employed several persons whom he trusted implicitly to execute his commissions in the ring. These men were never seen with Phil; in fact, they were practically strangers to the bookmakers. But they were a band of well-versed and thoroughly educated employees who learned signs and signals perfectly, which were directed from Phil while he sat apparently unconcerned in the grandstand, oblivious to what was going on in the betting ring. At the same time, his messenger, who was employed for such a purpose, kept Phil well posted as to the prices and who was betting on horses. It was not long before Sloan began winning race after race, and upon nearly every occasion, Phil's agents made some good-sized collections. All the wagers were made with cash. To blind the operations, each agent took a different section of the ring daily, so that the same bettor would not be so familiar to the bookmakers.

Before every race, Phil's commissioners would be at several points of vantage where they could catch his signals. Then they would go into the ring and fulfill his orders. Many of these commissioners were not known to each other, so secretly and systematically were the speculations accomplished. In less than three weeks, Phil had recovered all his previous losses and was a good winner. At the end of the first month, he was between $70,000 and $80,000 ahead.

The bookmakers were confused. They did not know where all the money was going to. None of the regulars seemed to be making any headway, and yet money was being taken out of the ring by strangers that no one knew except in a betting and collecting way. It was common to hear conversations between the bookmakers as they returned from the track, asking each other what they knew about that clerical looking fellow who beat three or four races that day, or that country looking chap who thought nothing of betting five or six hundred on a 3 to 1 shot, and collecting four times out of five.

Sloan was becoming so popular at the end of a month that he was a public favorite. The rank and file would have nothing but Sloan.

One day going home in the streetcar, Phil happened to be seated beside John Coleman, one of the most prominent and gentlemanly bookmakers in the business, when the conversation turned to the doings in the betting ring. "I can't understand who is getting all the money," said Coleman. "In the last month, I have lost over $10,000 and it has been split up into a thousand parts. No one man has got it; it has been divided between half a dozen big bettors whom nobody knows. They come along and bet two or three hundred in cash and invariably get away with it. There must be some big combination somewhere that is getting a lot of money. It reminds me of the 'Little Pete' episode of a few years ago when he had all the jockeys in the business on a string. The strangest part of the thing is that in nearly all cases, they play Sloan's mounts just as if he had been nominated to win every race no matter what horse he rides."

Phil smiled and intimated that Sloan was a good rider and no one could be blamed for following him.

"Well, in the future," replied Coleman, "if Sloan is on a natural 3 to 1 shot, they won't get better than 6 to 5 for my money. I think I'll string with them instead of going against the deluge of Sloan money, and there is many another bookmaker will do the same thing."

This was the beginning of the end of the successful campaign of the Phil-Sloan combination at Bay District track. When Phil saw that he would have to take such short prices against Sloan's mounts, he knew that the odds were somewhat against him. He knew it would eventually become unprofitable to accept even money against a horse that, under normal conditions, would be quoted at two or even three to one.

It was only a matter of a day or so when Phil settled up his affairs, paid off his commissioners, and packed his grip for the East, taking Sloan with him. Not until after he was gone did the bookmakers awaken, rub their eyes, and gradually grasp the fact that they had been outwitted by Pittsburgh Phil. In argument, some said that Phil had only just engaged Sloan to ride for him in the East on account of his good work in California. They were loath to believe that he had been in his employ for a month. It was not until the story was told by Phil himself that the skeptical could be made to understand that such a clever yet honorable system could have been employed to separate them from their bankrolls.

Sloan had to thank George E. Smith—Pittsburgh Phil— for his rise in the turf world.

10
ANECDOTES CONCERNING MEN OF FAME WHO WAGERED HUGE SUMS

The English School of Plungers in the Victorian Era may be divided into two classes. First was the amateur or patrician plunger who was usually the owner of a large and influential stable, and who employed the most talented trainers, the most fashionable jockeys, and the most astute watchers of horses, or "touts," as they are styled in England.

These owners necessarily had great wealth at their command, and the majority of the great plungers of this era had inherited their tastes for racing and gambling through a long line of ancestors. Many of them had stables of racehorses while yet in their teens and, though most of them ran their horses under assumed names or the name of some willing relative, the rosters of Oxford and Cambridge Universities and even the public schools of Eton and Harrow had many winning owners yearly among their students. Up to 1860 when the Gambling

Act went into force, betting lists of the prevailing odds on all the more important turf events were openly posted.

Yearling books on the Derby were common, 100 to 1 on the field being the usual quotation. It was an easy matter for the owner of a promising yearling to back his horse for a small outlay to win him any sum he might desire. At the time he made the bet, which was always play or pay, the race would be some eighteen months in the future, but that did not deter him; and almost invariably, the makers of the larger books on the race had to cover at a loss. The Cheshire Cup, a handicap at 21/4 miles, was a favorite race for early speculation. It was possible to back a horse for a large amount before the entries closed, and necessarily long before either the weights or acceptances were declared.

In those days information was not so readily obtainable by the racing public as it is today. Stable works were most jealously guarded. The majority of the horses outside of those at Newmarket, Epsom and Malton were trained at country villages, away from all railways and on private grounds, to which access by any unauthorized stranger was not only a difficult but a dangerous matter. All employees were under the strictest surveillance, letters were scrutinized by the trainer, and telegraph offices were only in the larger towns. It was very difficult to convey any stable secrets to the list keepers, who were always willing to pay high prices for information as to a prominent stable's intentions in important races. Horses for the leading events were dispatched to and from their training quarters to the course in covered vans accompanied by prize fighters, and were never left unguarded for a single instant. All the hay, oats and water necessary were taken from home and were under lock and key.

The return home of the winner of an important race was the occasion of a great jubilee. Bon fires were lighted, church bells pealed, and the poor of the neighborhood were feasted to their heart's content. Even ministers of the gospel owned and raced horses. As late as 1874, the winner of the St. Leger, "Apology," was bred and raised by the Reverend J. S. King, though she ran as being the property of "Mr. Launde," his registered and assumed name.

Queen Victoria maintained a large breeding farm at Hampton Court, the yearlings of which were disposed of annually at auction. Both George IV and William IV owned and raced large stables, and all the more important race meetings such as Epsom, Goodwood and Ascot were invariably graced by the royal presence. Under such mentorship, racing speedily became the fashion, and thanks to the sportsmanlike efforts of His Majesty, King Edward, is now on a higher plane in England than ever before. He is the breeder and owner of two Derby winners, Persimmon and Diamond Jubilee. Whenever his state duties permit, His Majesty journeys to the course for recreation, especially at Newmarket, where he mingles with the crowd as democratic and unguarded as an ordinary citizen. King Edward formerly dearly loved to "back his opinion;" and while he would not bet personally, the royal commission was executed by Captain Batchelor.

LADY ELIZABETH AND HERMIT

Among the plunges in the 60's, that of the Marquis of Hastings on his mare, Lady Elizabeth, was by far the most gigantic. It was an ill-fated one, as the mare showed nothing like her two-year-old form. Mr. Henry Chaplin, who owned Hermit, the Derby winner of 1867, is credited with winning the largest amount on that race of any individual. His winnings totaled $900,000, of which amount the Marquis of Hastings largely contributed as, in addition to being a backer, the Marquis made a large book among his friends on the race

in question. As Hermit started at the remunerative price of 66 to 1, the initial outlay to win this large sum was not so great.

The race in question was a memorable one as it was run in a blinding snowstorm. The Marquis considerably overlaid his book about Hermit to Chaplin, a matter of sentiment being the cause of the bitter feeling between the men. It was generally believed that the trouble between them was caused by a love affair. In order to meet his losses, the Marquis had to invoke the aid of Mr. Padwick, the fashionable moneylender of the day. His losses on this race probably equaled $600,000. He died at the early age of twenty-four, presumably of a broken heart. Outwardly cool but with an intensity of purpose that would not be denied, on several occasions he made the leading bookmakers stop laying against his own horse or that of a friend.

Lord Dupplin, who owned Petrarch, the winner of the 2,000 Guineas, was a very heavy plunger in the early 70's. His horses were trained by the shrewd Captain Machell, who probably brought off more coups than any of his professional brethren. Among the patrons of his stable were such plungers as the late Duke of Beaufort and the late Duke of Hamilton, the latter of whom is credited with losing over $5,000,000 on the turf.

The Duke of Beaufort confined his operations to flat racing only and, during a turf career of forty years, was only fortunate enough to own two really good horses, Ceylon and Petronel. The Duke of Hamilton maintained two large stables and was possibly more fond of a huge speculation on a steeplechase or hurdle race, than on a flat race, especially so when the King's present trainer, Richard Marsh, was wearing the ducal livery of "Cerise and French Grey" sleeves and cap. His turf losses became so excessive that he was compelled to dispose of the wonderful collection of pictures and objects of art in Hamilton Palace. This was a most remarkable sale that lasted four days and realized some $2,500,000. The catalogues of the sale cost each intending purchaser $5.00. Over six feet in height, with broad shoulders and a very red face, the Duke was easily distinguishable at most meetings. He invariably wore a blue shirt, which earned for him the sobriquet of the "Butcher Duke." Jack Wafts was his favorite flat race jockey, and possibly no incident of the great rider's turf career, outside of his victory in the Derby of '96 on Persimmon in the royal livery, gave that jockey half the satisfaction that he experienced when he beat Foxhall on the Duke's Fiddler at Ascot, the Duke winning very heavily on the race. An enormous amount was taken out of the ring when the Duke's horse Ossian won the St. Leger of '83.

SIR GEORGE CHETWYND AND SIR JOHN ASHLEY

Sir George Chetwynd and Sir John Ashley were the owners of large stables from 1870 to 1880. Both of these baronets had calls upon the riding services of Charlie Woods. Many a successful coup was landed by the confederacy until the jockey lost his license, through complicity in the ownership of horses in conjunction with Sir George Chetwynd and Sir John Ashley. The latter was the patron of all manly sports and was the owner of Peter and other celebrities. Thanks to the wonderful efforts of Archer, who persuaded that erratic horse to try again when he stopped to kick during the race for the Royal Hunt Cup, eventually finished first, the owner won an enormous sum on the result.

Sir John also won a tremendous amount on Scamp when the horse won the International Hurdle Race, one of the then leading cross country events. Scamp won a Goodwood Cup as well, and was sent to Australia where he sired some good winners. Always cheery, with his broad brimmed derby hat on one side of his head, a huge cigar in his mouth and wearing the invariable red necktie, Sir John's advent at the rail of Tattersall's ring was always the prelude for some heavy wagers to be recorded well up in the thousands. He had a large stable in training and the somewhat doubtful distinction of winning more selling races than any other owner in the course of the year. Sir John was an athlete of no mean ability and on one occasion took the law into his own hands and administered a severe beating to Plunger Walton, the whilom American turf speculator, whom he accused of seeking information from his jockey.

THE BROTHERS BALTAZZI

Two young Hungarians, the brothers Baltazzi, flashed upon the English turf in 1875 and soon had a stable upon which great plunges were made in 1876. They had a very promising colt unnamed, which, throughout the winter betting on the Derby, had occasionally received support. Finding themselves in financial difficulties, they had to apply to the late Sam Lewis, the great turf moneylender of Cork Street, Picadilly, for assistance, giving as part security for the loan a bill of sale of their horses, among them the horse in question known then as the "Mineral Colt."

Failing to meet their obligations with Mr. Lewis, the latter sent for Mr. Baltazzi to ask him for a delivery order for the horses. Mr. Baltazzi was willing to turn them all over to him except the Mineral Colt, and tried hard to get Lewis to agree to except him, but Lewis said the colt was the only one that had any pretensions to class and he must insist upon receiving it.

Baltazzi then signed the order and hurled it at Lewis, bursting into tears as he did so. Lewis looked askance for a moment or two, and then asked, "What's the matter?"

"I had set my heart upon winning your English Derby and now the colt is yours," Baltazzi replied. "There is nothing to prevent your going to Tattersall's and scratching him."

"Do you really think the colt has a chance to win?" Lewis said, after some thought.

"Yes, a great chance," Baltazzi replied.

Lewis reached into a drawer, pulled out a cheque book, wrote a cheque to Baltazzi's order for a thousand pounds, and handed it to him. At the same time, he tore up the Bill of Sale, saying: "Well, if you really think he has a chance, put that on him and if you want any more, come back."

The colt did well and as history records, he won the Derby in 1876 in the hands of Custance, being named "Kisber" on the morning of the race after the Baltazzi Estate in Hungary. This victory well replenished the Baltazzi exchequer and, needless to say, Sam Lewis got more than his own. Unfortunately, their turf speculations were unwise and they returned to their native land, where they still operate a small stable.

JUBILEE JUGGINS AND OTHER PLUNGERS

Ernest Benzon of Birmingham, the only son of a Hebrew iron founder, flashed on the turf in 1887 and while not a patrician, he had something like one and a half million dollars in ready cash at his disposal. He first startled the turf world by betting $50,000 on Bendigo for the Jubilee Cup at Kempton. This plunge was successful and speedily earned for him the title, "The Jubilee Plunger." As the young man's dissipations speedily became notorious, it was changed to "Jubilee Juggins." He paid large prices for horses, but his stable was notoriously mismanaged and eventually he finished penniless and was sent to jail for debt.

While in prison he amused himself by writing a book of his life, which he entitled, "My Fortune and How I Spent It." It is more than probable that he lost more at cards and dice than he did on the turf. His other extravagances were numerous. One of his "fads" was never to wear the same shirt twice.

Of the professional plungers of humble origin who were in no instance helped by rich relatives, a few may be mentioned. Principal among them must be included John Hammond of Newmarket, who polished shoes and sold shoelaces as a boy in the streets of London. He next held a humble position in a stable and eventually became the owner of a large string of horses—and the heaviest speculator whose operations were conducted upon a businesslike basis. At one time a tout, Hammond naturally had a good eye for a horse, and through doing Fred Archer a slight service, eventually became that famous jockey's great friend. No doubt through Archer's information about the horses he rode, Hammond profited largely.

Hammond owned St. Gatien, who ran a dead heat with Harvester for the Derby; and also the great mare, Florence, by whose Cambridgeshire victory he is credited with winning $500,000. Eventually Archer and he had a quarrel and the jockey transferred his friendship to Arthur Cooper and Joseph Davis, the latter of whom was wealthy and who raced a stable. Eighteen months later, Hammond became penniless and again sold shoelaces.

Davis won a large amount when his horse Fortissimo won the Goodwood Stakes. In this event he was fortunate enough to secure Archer's services. Mr. Davis, who is the principal owner of Hurst Park, one of the most profitably run courses near London, never plunges now. Arthur Cooper, after amassing much wealth, was stricken with consumption and died some years ago.

Sam Lewis, when he found time to attend races, was a very large operator and would think nothing of betting from ten thousand to twenty thousand pounds in an afternoon.

THE OTHER ENGLISH RACE GOERS

There are hundreds of race goers in England who make good incomes yearly by backing horses, despite the increased cost of attending the meetings. Traveling and other expenses there are much higher than in the United States. It is by no means impossible to make money on the races, but to do so it is certainly incumbent that common sense, sobriety and a strict attention to every detail be followed.

Unnecessary extravagances are the rock upon which so many racetrack ships are shattered. The prices quoted against horses' chances seem to have a tremendous effect upon the average bettor. For instance, if the horse upon which one intends to place a wager is quoted at even money, 6 to 5, or 7 to 5, he says, "That is too short a price for me," and places his capital upon possibly the longest priced horse in the race.

On the other hand, when a horse that a bettor thinks should be 4 to 1 or 5 to 1 is quoted at 8 to 1 or 10 to 1, he turns to the favorite—and in both instances, he probably has the mortification of seeing his original choice the winner. "The chalk hurt me," has been the refrain of many a backer and is one that should never be allowed to influence an individual who has a good reason for making a wager.

"Any price is a good price if it is a winning one" is an old adage. "It is not the bets that win but those that lose that hurt" is another one.

11
DRUGS AND THEIR EFFECT UPON HORSES

One custom among owners and trainers of horses in this country has done more harm to racing then any other practice. It is the stimulation of horses before their races, the purpose being to make them exert themselves to the fullest extent. It is a custom that every racing association has tried to overcome, but, sorry to say, without complete success. Stimulating horses has been carried to such excess that there is a certain amount of suspicion attached to almost every horse that goes to the post, especially among the common lot.

It is not the use of a stimulant that is so much feared as the abuse of it. If an owner is consistent in its use, it can be tolerated, for anything that will make a horse run consistently is all that officials should desire. It is the inconsistent running of horses that creates scandal. There are horses that can run, but won't unless given some kind of stimulant, whether it be mild or forceful, much depending upon the temperament of the animal.

Some stimulants have just about the same effect upon horses as a cocktail upon a human being. One cocktail is often sufficient to oil up the good humor and knowledge of a person that otherwise would not be brought out, while it will take ten times that quantity to have the same effect upon another person. So it is with stimulating horses. And while some drugs will have the desired effect upon one horse, they will act in a decidedly different manner upon others.

It is all a question of temperament and physical condition of the subject. Hence it is that a thorough knowledge of administering a stimulant is required, as well as a thorough knowledge of the disposition of a horse. To diagnose the traits of a horse properly, many experiments must necessarily be tried. Once a satisfactory result has been ascertained, a trainer knows just what drug is best for the disposition of the animal and how to use it.

It is the lack of this knowledge and the careless use of stimulants that cause horses to become positively uncontrollable. In many cases, horses have been known to run until they fall exhausted and in more than one instance, have died on the track. Stimulating has had bad effects after a race if an overdose has been applied, or if a stimulant has been administered that did not act in accord with the physical make up of the animal.

If given a powerful stimulant, a high strung, nervous, ill-tempered horse will act much as an individual who possesses the same sort of disposition and has drunk too freely of liquor. He will want to fight and break everything in sight. The horse will desire to run and not stop until nature is exhausted. This does not infer that every horse that has run away with a jockey has been stimulated, as there are some horses crazy enough to do almost anything in the line of contrariness.

What the speculator on horse racing wants to know is to be able to tell when a horse is stimulated or not. In these days of science and the constant attention horsemen have paid to the stimulating question, it is safe to assert that even the most experienced veterinarians are at times deceived by the condition of a horse and cannot always detect the use of stimulants. In experimenting, veterinarians have administered a certain stimulant to a horse, raced him, and after investigation, have found nothing out of the ordinary in the cooling out process. In fact, the animal returned to his stall normal in every way except for a natural increase in heart action and temperature, which is to be expected after a severe effort of any kind in horse or man.

A veterinarian who is conversant with all the tricks of the stimulating process has made public much desirable information on the subject, which is quoted in his exact language. He has described all the drugs that were used. It is not necessary to enumerate them here. For the information of the majority, it is believed expedient to enlighten them as to the effects that certain drugs have on horses and how they can be outwardly observed if a careful search is made.

THE VETERINARIAN'S REPORT ON STIMULANTS

"Stimulating horses—or as it is vulgarly called, 'doping' or 'hopping—has been in vogue in America for a great number of years," this celebrated veterinarian said. "My earliest recollection was at Clifton, Guttenberg and Gloucester, when these were famous winter meetings. I have seen it also at various minor meetings.

"There is no doubt in my mind that an animal so highly sensitive and of such a temperament as the thoroughbred can be made, by the judicious use of stimulants, to do his utmost when called upon. Here it is where one trainer who has a knowledge of the action and uses of stimulants has an advantage over his brother trainer who does not possess such knowledge. All horses are not alike and the dose administered to one, which will be attended by the best results, may be a total failure in another animal.

"What I am shall endeavor to explain is how a person who is not an expert may know whether the animal is stimulated or not. Various drugs produce various symptoms. I will now try to explain how and when to tell that an animal has been stimulated.

"You enter the enclosure or paddock, where the finishing touches are given previous to going to the post. The first thing you look for is the expression you see in the eyes of a horse. If he has an animated look—eyes bright and dilated with a look of expectancy about him, is restless with nostrils dilated, is perspiring or sweating (the latter may only be slight), is excitable, and in fact, acts and looks as if he were in a very anxious mood—you can safely infer that a stimulant has been administered.

"You must not mistake a nervous, high strung, excitable animal for one that has been given a stimulant. The nervous animal does not have that anxious, expectant look. He has a wild or scared expression. He may be perspiring freely, but it is not always a sign of stimulation with him. If watched closely, you will invariably find the animal's bowels move very often. This is due to the excitement attendant upon his nervous temperament induced by his surroundings.

"Look carefully over a horse you believe is stimulated and observe if there is any froth or saliva about his mouth; if so, he has had heroin, which is given on the tongue. One of its symptoms is the frothing saliva or drooling. The attendant frequently keeps sponging his mouth as he walks around, hoping to divert attention from the saliva.

"Take a look at the next horse walking around the paddock, very calm and taking no notice of his surroundings.

Do not be fooled (he too has been stimulated), but it takes a thorough horseman and an expert to discover it. This animal has a stimulant to which codeine, which checks the excitable propensities, has been added.

"Some animals are more easily affected than others. It was to this knowledge, acquired by some noted plungers, that their success was due. They were able to tell when an animal was so stimulated by having an expert in their employ who could invariably detect the fact at a glance. I know a well-known veterinarian who was often sent into the paddock to give his opinion, and large wagers were made on or against the animal according to his judgment.

"The system of stimulating animals is in universal practice, nearly all stables from the highest to the lowest using every known means to animate their charges and make them do their utmost. Trainers contrive to get the best prescriptions that can be relied upon to give extra stamina and endurance, and also to cause the animal to do his best without unduly exciting him."

COMMON DRUGS USED TO STIMULATE HORSES

"The following drugs are the most common ones used in the practice of stimulation: cocaine, caffeine, codeine, coffee, digitalis, strychnine, nux vomica, strophanthus, kola, heroin, sherry, whiskey, brandy, and last though not least, nitroglycerine. The following will give an idea how these various drugs have been and are used.

"The earliest system by which the animal was stimulated was by giving a strong drench of coffee about one-half hour before post time, or a pint of sherry, whiskey or brandy. Later came the hypodermic with which doses of cocaine, varying from 1½ to 15 grains, was introduced by the needle under the animal's skin just before he went to the post. There were no paddock judges then and such measures were used without fear of detection.

"Now all is changed, the skillful trainer tries that which will be least noticed except to the trained and observant expert. He hunts up all kinds of formulas, discusses the pros and cons with his brothers in the profession, and administers a stimulant to the animal under his charge that will give the best results and is as little noticeable as possible. Sometimes the dose given is too strong. The animal either wears himself out in the paddock or at the post, or runs away with the jockey. Very often, an overdose will take the animal's speed away. Many unscrupulous trainers employ this method where they wish to retard speed. The horse will stop to a walk, as it were, when he is called upon for a final struggle.

"Cocaine is very extensively used, the muriate being the salt preferred. This is a great cerebral stimulant producing mental excitement. Its action upon the circulation is pronounced, though less than on the nervous system. Codeine is used where there is a very nervous excitable animal. It is obtained from opium. While it quiets, its action does not interfere with speed or endurance.

"Digitalis exerts great power over the circulation, the work done by the heart under its influence being far more than normal. It is slow in its action and is generally given in conjunction with other agents. Strychnine and nux vomica are identical in their action. They are great stimulants of the brain and spinal cord, but seem to have greater effect when used with other drugs.

"Strophanthus in moderate doses is a stimulant. In large doses, it retards the speed. Capsicum is used as a base for other agents. Kola and its preparations are largely used. The powdered kola nut is used in capsules with other ingredients. The fluid extract, however, is the most used preparation.

"The muriate of heroin is a salt generally used, and it is placed on the tongue. Also used in conjunction with other drugs, heroin can be detected by frothing at the mouth and a continuous scraping of the tongue against the upper teeth. Nitroglycerine (spirits of glonoin) is one of the best heart stimulants known. It is always given with other agents, thus increasing its action.

"If a horse going to the post has an animated look, eyes are bright and expectant, moves in a brisk, jaunty manner, and is slightly breaking out or sweating, he is under the influence of some stimulant. Kola, cocaine, digitalis or strychnine, or a mixture of them, will produce these symptoms. There comes another one that does not have that bright, jaunty air about him, but around his mouth there is saliva or froth. He champs his bit and is sweating slightly. By the time he gets to the post, he may be in a lather. In that case, heroin has been used. No matter how it is used, either by itself or in conjunction with other drugs, heroin has this infallible sign.

"Another horse may be nervous or excited, but the muscles of his chest and thighs are shivering as if he were cold. Rely upon it that he has been stimulated with either cocaine, strychnine and digitalis combined, or alone. Any of these will produce these symptoms. Another that shows no excitability or nervousness, is not even breaking out, has no animated look about him, may be stimulated with codeine and other stimulants combined that take a longer time to work. He is kept working in the paddock, and his jockey is told to keep him moving about at the post and very often is given instructions to canter him there. When you see an animal as dry as a bone, to use a slang term, no animation about him, he either has not been stimulated or he has been given something such as strophanthus that will retard his effort to do his utmost."

12

AN EXPLANATION OF THE TIME AND WEIGHT PERCENTAGE TABLE

The time and weight schedule that is published herein does not necessarily belong in the work, as Pittsburgh Phil rarely depended upon time for his deductions. However, as it is believed to be a help of no little importance to those who are interested in turf affairs, it was considered not out of place to render as much assistance and knowledge as possible in estimating the relative merits of horses.

The origin of the accompanying schedule system is a problem. Some say that it is the Australian system of classifying horses, others credit its production to a man named Gale; but no matter who the originator may have been, it has been a source of valuable deductions to many who have been fortunate enough to possess it and who have taken the trouble to abide by its results.

It has been proven beyond doubt that its figures will indicate the best horses in races to an overwhelming degree,

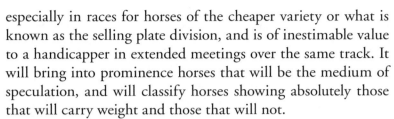
especially in races for horses of the cheaper variety or what is known as the selling plate division, and is of inestimable value to a handicapper in extended meetings over the same track. It will bring into prominence horses that will be the medium of speculation, and will classify horses showing absolutely those that will carry weight and those that will not.

It is a simple study, one taking little or no time to keep in touch with, so far as the record is concerned, but much knowledge of existing conditions and horses is required to bring about a final conclusion. In other words, it will point directly to the best horses in a race, after which subtractions and additions must be made before speculating upon the result.

The method to arrive at a percentage figure for a certain horse is simple. Distances are given in the table for races at every given point from three furlongs up to two miles, and a percentage is attached to each distance, beginning with a foundation of .300 and reduced to .180, with fractional time figures to line up with the percentage figures. In this respect, it is simply a time table showing what credit percentage a horse should be given if it runs a certain distance in a specified time. To get at this, one must get the distance of the race from the head of the table and move his finger downward to the time in which the race was run, then glance to the left, and gather the percentage figure from the left end of the line.

For instance, if a horse runs a mile in 1.40 ¼, its percentage would be .282. Should a horse run six furlongs in 1.13 ¾, the percentage figure would be .273. After getting the percentage figure, one should record it in his book of race records or form chart. The percentage indicated only alludes to the winning horses. Deductions have to be made for those that finish in the rear to get at their respective values. You can obtain these deductions by adding and subtracting points for pounds, distances and time. For instance, if a horse winning a race shows a percentage of .282, which would be a mile in 1.40 ¼, and the nearest horse to him was three lengths away, nine points would be deducted from .282, thus making the percentage of the second horse .273, three points being deducted for each length that a horse is beaten.

Allowances must be made, however, in cases where a horse is not fully extended and where, in the judgment of the handicapper, the horse could have done better. A horse may finish three lengths from a winner, yet he may be eased up owing to a wide margin between him and the third horse. In such cases, the judgment of the handicappers must be brought into play. Should all horses be extended, you can rely upon the rule of allowing three points to a length in all races at a mile and over. In races less than a mile, an allowance of two points to the length and two points to the quarter of a second has brought about more definite results.

The general rule applied to the table is to calculate an allowance or penalty of three points to a length, three points to a quarter of a second, and one point to a pound as the case may be. A horse that runs a mile in 1.40 would be credited with three points less in percentage than the horse that runs a mile in 1.39 ¾, providing the weight is the same and the atmospheric and track conditions are normal in both cases. The latter, of course, is a matter of judgment. These figures indicate that the horse running the fastest mile would beat the 1.40 horse by a length in a truly run race—and it must always be presumed that the race will be truly run unless technical conditions enter into the argument, such as one horse being a slow beginner and more likely to meet with interference than his opponent, and similar incidents in connection with a race.

What this table will show positively is the ability of some horses to carry weight better than others. It will be frequently discovered that a horse will run six furlongs, or in fact any distance within reason, in as fast a time with weight up as he will with the proverbial "feather on his back." This indicates class and will bring out decided choices in high weight races. A horse with light weight up will run a phenomenal race one day and will beat a correspondingly lightly weighted opponent. But put the same two horses in a race the next day, and let each pick up in the neighborhood of twenty pounds, and the positions and running of the horses will possibly be decidedly reversed, the one being a good weight carrier, while the other is anchored with anything but a light impost.

In conclusion, the schedule will bring the best horses to the top of the list of entries in a race if deductions are made from their best races and at distances suitable to them. It will distinctly indicate horses that run good races carrying high weights. And it will show a class of horses that cannot carry weight to advantage, and point directly to the weight they are physically fitted to carry. It will classify horses by showing a high percentage in races where high weights predominate. It will also possess other advantages that will be discovered if studied closely.

One thing must never be forgotten before arriving at a conclusion—a horse may show a very high percentage when racing against horses of his own class such as, for instance, a selling plater against selling platers carrying 110 pounds each. With clear sailing and every advantage, the winner might run six furlongs in 1.13, which would give him a percentage of .282. This same horse might be asked to meet handicap horses a few days later and only be handicapped with 90 pounds, which would then give him a figure of .302 in the percentage column.

Figuring the time in which he should run the race to a minimum, at an allowance of three points to a quarter of a second, he would be expected to run six furlongs with 90 pounds up at least one second and a half faster than he did in the race a few days before with 110 pounds up. This would make him finish the distance by 1.111/2 on cold calculation. Such a performance is hardly probable. In fact, it is more than probable that he would be beaten in a slower time than 1.13 as he met a better class of horses, which records will prove is the result of such contests in the majority of cases.

Class always predominates when other conditions are normal. This must always be taken into consideration, as well as the existing condition of every horse running in a race, before arriving at a conclusion in trying to ascertain the winner, no matter what system of figuring is employed.

TIME AND WEIGHT PERCENTAGE TABLE

	2 miles	1 7/8	1 3/4	1 5/8	1 1/2	1 3/8	1 1/4	B.C.	1 3/16	1 1/8	1 1/16	1.100	1.70	1.50	1.20	1 mile	7 1/2	7/8	6 1/2	3/4	S.C.	5 1/2	5/8	4 1/2	1/2	3 1/2	3/8
300	3/4	3/4	3/4	3/4	3/4	3/4	3/4	3/4	3/4	3/4	3/4	145	143	142	140	3/4	3/4	125	119	112	108	105	59	53	46	1/4	1/2
297	331	317	303	249	235	221	207	202	200	153	146	1/4	1/4	1/4	1/4	139	132	1/4	1/4	1/4	1/4	1/4	1/4	1/4	1/4	1/2	3/4
294	3/4	3/4	3/4	3/4	3/4	3/4	3/4	3/4	3/4	3/4	1/4	1/2	1/2	1/2	1/2	1/4	1/4	1/2	1/2	1/2	1/2	1/2	1/2	1/2	1/2	3/4	35
291	1/2	1/4	1/2	1/4	1/2	1/4	1/4	1/4	1/4	1/2	1/2	3/4	3/4	3/4	3/4	1/2	1/2	3/4	3/4	3/4	3/4	3/4	3/4	3/4	3/4	41	1/4
288	3/4	3/4	3/4	3/4	3/4	3/4	3/4	3/4	3/4	3/4	3/4	146	144	143	141	3/4	3/4	126	120	113	109	106	100	54	47	1/4	1/2
285	332	318	304	250	236	222	208	203	201	154	147	1/4	1/4	1/4	1/4	140	133	1/4	1/4	1/4	1/4	1/4	1/4	1/4	1/4	1/2	3/4
282	1/4	1/4	1/4	1/4	1/4	1/4	1/4	1/4	1/4	1/4	1/4	1/2	1/2	1/2	1/2	1/4	1/4	1/2	1/2	1/2	1/2	1/2	1/2	1/2	1/2	3/4	36
279	1/2	3/4	1/2	1/2	1/2	1/2	1/2	1/2	1/2	1/2	1/2	3/4	3/4	3/4	3/4	1/2	1/2	3/4	3/4	3/4	3/4	3/4	3/4	3/4	3/4	42	1/4
276	3/4	3/4	3/4	3/4	3/4	3/4	3/4	3/4	3/4	3/4	3/4	147	145	144	142	3/4	3/4	127	121	114	110	107	101	55	48	1/4	1/2
273	333	319	305	251	237	223	209	204	202	155	148	1/4	1/4	1/4	1/4	141	134	1/4	1/4	1/4	1/4	1/4	1/4	1/4	1/4	1/2	3/4
270	1/4	3/4	1/4	1/4	1/4	1/4	1/4	1/4	1/4	1/4	1/4	1/2	1/2	1/2	1/2	1/4	1/4	1/2	1/2	1/2	1/2	1/2	1/2	1/2	1/2	3/4	37
267	1/2	1/4	1/2	1/2	1/2	1/2	1/2	1/2	1/2	1/2	1/2	3/4	3/4	3/4	3/4	1/2	1/2	3/4	3/4	3/4	3/4	3/4	3/4	3/4	3/4	43	1/4
264	3/4	3/4	3/4	3/4	3/4	3/4	3/4	3/4	3/4	3/4	3/4	148	146	145	143	3/4	3/4	128	122	115	111	108	102	56	49	1/4	1/2
261	334	320	306	252	238	224	210	205	203	156	149	1/4	1/4	1/4	1/4	142	135	1/4	1/4	1/4	1/4	1/4	1/4	1/4	1/4	1/2	3/4
258	1/4	1/4	1/4	1/4	1/4	1/4	1/4	1/4	1/4	1/4	1/4	1/2	1/2	1/2	1/2	1/4	1/4	1/2	1/2	1/2	1/2	1/2	1/2	1/2	1/2	3/4	38
255	1/2	1/2	1/2	1/2	1/2	1/2	1/2	1/2	1/2	1/2	1/2	3/4	3/4	3/4	3/4	1/2	1/2	3/4	3/4	3/4	3/4	3/4	3/4	3/4	3/4	44	1/4
252	3/4	3/4	3/4	3/4	3/4	3/4	3/4	3/4	3/4	3/4	3/4	149	147	146	144	3/4	3/4	129	123	116	112	109	103	57	50	1/4	1/2
249	335	321	307	253	239	225	211	206	204	157	150	1/4	1/4	1/4	1/4	143	136	1/4	1/4	1/4	1/4	1/4	1/4	1/4	1/4	1/2	3/4
246	1/4	1/4	1/4	1/4	1/4	1/4	1/4	1/4	1/4	1/4	1/4	1/2	1/2	1/2	1/2	1/4	1/4	1/2	3/4	1/4	3/4	3/4	3/4	1/2	1/2	3/4	39
243	1/2	1/2	1/2	1/2	1/2	1/2	1/2	1/2	1/2	1/2	1/2	3/4	3/4	3/4	3/4	1/2	1/2	3/4		3/4				3/4	3/4	45	1/4

THE TIME & WEIGHT PERCENTAGE TABLE

	240	237	234	231	228	225	222	219	216	213	210	207	204	201	198	195	192	189	186	183	180
2 miles	3/4	336	1/4	1/2	3/4	337	1/4	1/2	3/4	338	1/4	1/2	3/4	339	1/4	1/2	3/4	340	1/4	1/2	3/4
1 7/8	3/4	322	1/4	1/2	3/4	323	1/4	1/2	3/4	324	1/4	1/2	3/4	325	1/4	1/2	3/4	326	1/4	1/2	3/4
1 3/4	3/4	308	1/4	1/2	3/4	309	1/4	1/2	3/4	310	1/4	1/2	3/4	311	1/4	1/2	3/4	312	1/4	1/2	3/4
1 5/8	3/4	254	1/4	1/2	3/4	255	1/4	1/2	3/4	256	1/4	1/2	3/4	257	1/4	1/2	3/4	258	1/4	1/2	3/4
1 1/2	3/4	240	1/4	1/2	3/4	241	1/4	1/2	3/4	242	1/4	1/2	3/4	243	1/4	1/2	3/4	244	1/4	1/2	3/4
1 3/8	3/4	226	1/4	1/2	3/4	227	1/4	1/2	3/4	228	1/4	1/2	3/4	229	1/4	1/2	3/4	230	1/4	1/2	3/4
1 1/4	3/4	212	1/4	1/2	3/4	213	1/4	1/2	3/4	214	1/4	1/2	3/4	215	1/4	1/2	3/4	216	1/4	1/2	3/4
B.C.	3/4	207	1/4	1/2	3/4	208	1/4	1/2	3/4	209	1/4	1/2	3/4	210	1/4	1/2	3/4	211	1/4	1/2	3/4
1 3/16	3/4	205	1/4	1/2	3/4	206	1/4	1/2	3/4	207	1/4	1/2	3/4	208	1/4	1/2	3/4	209	1/4	1/2	3/4
1 1/8	3/4	158	1/4	1/2	3/4	159	1/4	1/2	3/4	160	1/4	1/2	3/4	161	1/4	1/2	3/4	162	1/4	1/2	3/4
1 1/16	3/4	151	1/4	1/2	3/4	152	1/4	1/2	3/4	153	1/4	1/2	3/4	154	1/4	1/2	3/4	155	1/4	1/2	3/4
1.100	150	1/4	1/2	3/4	151	1/4	1/2	3/4	152	1/4	1/2	3/4	153	1/4	1/2	3/4	154	1/4	1/2	3/4	155
1.70	148	1/4	1/2	3/4	149	1/4	1/2	3/4	150	1/4	1/2	3/4	151	1/4	1/2	3/4	152	1/4	1/2	3/4	153
1.50	147	1/4	1/2	3/4	148	1/4	1/2	3/4	149	1/4	1/2	3/4	150	1/4	1/2	3/4	151	1/4	1/2	3/4	152
1.20	145	1/4	1/2	3/4	146	1/4	1/2	3/4	147	1/4	1/2	3/4	148	1/4	1/2	3/4	149	1/4	1/2	3/4	150
1 mile	3/4	144	1/4	1/2	3/4	145	1/4	1/2	3/4	146	1/4	1/2	3/4	147	1/4	1/2	3/4	148	1/4	1/2	3/4
7 1/2	3/4	137	1/4	1/2	3/4	138	1/4	1/2	3/4	139	1/4	1/2	3/4	140	1/4	1/2	3/4	141	1/4	1/2	3/4
7/8	130	1/4	1/2	3/4	131	1/4	1/2	3/4	132	1/4	1/2	3/4	133	1/4	1/2	3/4	134	1/4	1/2	3/4	135
6 1/2	1/4	1/2	3/4	124	1/4	1/2	3/4	125	1/4	1/2	3/4	126	1/4	1/2	3/4	127	1/4	1/2	3/4	128	1/4
3/4	1/2	3/4	117	1/4	1/2	3/4	118	1/4	1/2	3/4	119	1/4	1/2	3/4	120	1/4	1/2	3/4	121	1/4	1/2
S.C.	1/4	1/2	3/4	113	1/4	1/2	3/4	114	1/4	1/2	3/4	115	1/4	1/2	3/4	116	1/4	1/2	3/4	117	1/4
5 1/2	110	1/4	1/2	3/4	111	1/4	1/2	3/4	112	1/4	1/2	3/4	113	1/4	1/2	3/4	114	1/4	1/2	3/4	115
5/8	1/2	3/4	104	1/4	1/2	3/4	105	1/4	1/2	3/4	106	1/4	1/2	3/4	107	1/4	1/2	3/4	108	1/4	1/2
4 1/2	1/4	1/2	3/4	58	1/4	1/2	3/4	59	1/4	1/2	3/4	60	1/4	1/2	3/4	61	1/4	1/2	3/4	62	1/4
1/2	51	1/4	1/2	3/4	52	1/4	1/2	3/4	53	1/4	1/2	3/4	54	1/4	1/2	3/4	55	1/4	1/2	3/4	56
3 1/2	1/4	1/2	3/4	46	1/4	1/2	3/4	47	1/4	1/2	3/4	48	1/4	1/2	3/4	49	1/4	1/2	3/4	50	1/4
3/8	1/2	3/4	40	1/4	1/2	3/4	41	1/4	1/2	3/4	42	1/4	1/2	3/4	43	1/4	1/2	3/4	44	1/4	1/2

13
MAXIMS OF
PITTSBURGH PHIL: PART 1

☞ A good jockey, a good horse, a good bet.

☞ A poor jockey, a good horse, a moderate bet.

☞ A good horse, a moderate jockey, a moderate bet.

☞ A man who plays the races successfully must have opinions of his own and the strength to stick to them no matter what he hears.

☞ Successful handicappers know every detail regarding the horses upon which they intend to place their money.

☞ The minute that a man loses his balance on the racetrack he is like a horse that is trying to run away.

☞ A man cannot divide his attention at the track between horses and women.

☞ All consistently successful players of horses are men of temperate habits in life.

☞ The racing man should arise in the morning cool and clear headed and should then take up the problem of the day.

☞ Some horses will run good races over certain tracks, while in the same company under similar conditions on other tracks, they will run very disappointingly. Study the likes and dislikes of a horse in regard to tracks.

☞ If there are two or three very fast horses in a race, one or two of them will quit before the end of the journey. Hence, look out for your intelligent jockey.

☞ Many killings are attempted. Few are accomplished.

☞ In handicaps, the top weights are always at a disadvantage unless they are very high-class horses.

☞ Few trainers can send a horse to the post the first time out in perfect condition.

☞ One race for a horse is equal to two or three private trials.

☞ Horses are the same as human beings where condition is the test of superiority.

☞ Winners repeat frequently while the defeated are apt to be defeated almost continuously.

☞ The majority of horses will go further over the turf than they will over the dirt course. Mud runners are usually good on the turf.

14
MAXIMS OF
PITTSBURGH PHIL: PART 2

☞ Time enters into the argument under certain conditions, but if depended upon entirely for a deduction, it will be found wanting.

☞ The ability to tell whether a horse is at its best before a race is acquired only after years of the closest kind of study.

☞ Special knowledge is not a talent. A man must acquire it by hard work.

☞ A horse that frets is a very dangerous betting proposition.

☞ The majority of the riders and horses are game and will fight for victory no matter where they are placed.

☞ Some jockeys excel on heavy tracks.

☞ A good mud rider will frequently bring a bad horse home.

☞ You cannot be a successful horseplayer if you get the worst of the price all the time.

☞ The basis of all speculation is the amount of profit to be obtained on an investment.

☞ Learn to finance your money to advantage.

☞ The clocker is something like the scout in the army.

☞ Honest horses ridden by honest boys are sometimes beaten by honest trainers. Though intended to be for the best, instructions are sometimes given to the riders that mean sure defeat.

☞ The resistance of the wind is very great in a horse race, and it is correspondingly great when acting as a propeller. Wind and atmosphere have considerable effect on horses that are troubled in their respiratory organs.

☞ Class in a horse is the ability it possesses to carry its stipulated stake weight, take the track, and go the distance that nature intended it should go.

☞ I figure that two-year-olds can give considerably more weight away to horses in their class than can horses in the older division, except in isolated areas.

☞ There is enough natural inconsistency in horse racing without having it forced upon the public by unscrupulous men, yet there is not one-tenth of one per cent as much crookedness on the turf as it is given credit for.

☞ A horse that is not contented in its stable cannot take on flesh and be happy.

☞ Every horse I ever owned improved after I had him long enough to study his disposition.

15
MAXIMS OF PITTSBURGH PHIL: PART 3

☞ A horse expects to race if he is a thoroughbred, just the same as a game chicken is anxious to fight.

☞ When you feel yourself getting out of form, take a rest and freshen up.

☞ What is frequently right in form is wrong in condition. If a horse is not in good condition, he might as well be in the stable.

☞ Look for improvement of mares in the fall of the year. They train better and are more consistent.

☞ There are mud riders as well as mud runners in the racing world.

☞ A jockey should not be overloaded with instructions.

☞ It is not bad speculation to pick out two or three sure-looking bets and parlay a small amount.

☞ Cut your bets when in a losing streak. Increase them when running in a spasm of good luck.

☞ Double your wages when you have the bookmakers' money in hand.

☞ It is not always the heaviest commission that is collected. The weight of the commission does not make a horse win. A poor man's horse and his $10 speak as loudly as a $10,000 commission from a millionaire. It is the horse that must be considered.

☞ Condition has more to do with a horse winning or losing a race than the weight it carries.

☞ A horse in poor condition cannot beat one of his own class.

☞ A high-class horse cannot win a race with a feather on his back if he is not in condition.

☞ Watch all the horses racing closely. You may see something that will be of benefit later on.

☞ It is as well to play horses that are in winning form. A horse in winning condition generally repeats or runs into the money.

☞ Different tracks frequently cause decided changes in form. Study horses' whims and fancies for certain tracks and you will see a good lay or a good play. A high-class horse will do his best on any track.

☞ The less one thinks of crookedness and trickery in racing the more successful will be his handicapping.

☞ Look for defect in your own calculating rather than cheating in others.

☞ Know when to put a good bet down and when not to.

ATTENTION: HORSE PLAYERS!

If you like this book, come to our website, and browse our extensive library of titles—we not only have the world's largest selection of horse titles (*more than 25 times* the selection of major chain superstores), but over 3,000 total gaming and gambling titles!